THE
EYES OF
HONOR

The Currency of Heaven

Dr. Gene Herndon

AiON MULTIMEDIA
"The Word is Eternal" Isaiah 40:8

Published by Aion Multimedia

20118 N 67th Ave

Suite 300-446

Glendale, AZ 85308

www.aionmultimedia.com

ISBN-13: 978-1-7330332-3-7

Table of Contents

CHAPTER 1:

INTRUDING

People in today's Western world don't recognize the concept of Honor. Honor is a lost art, and I believe the main reason most people struggle is that they have not developed a life of honor. We're going to talk about the Eyes/I's of Honor, and the Eyes/I's of Dishonor.

Galatians 3:9 says:

> **So then they which be of faith are blessed with faithful Abraham.**

The blessing is located between "Faith" and "Faithfulness." Most of the time, particularly in the universal body of Christ, people who talk about prospering and about blessings talk about these things as if they're promises only, and not part of a covenant. The nature of a covenant is that there is a requirement on both sides; any relationship without reciprocity will die. For example, let's say I meet the Curry Family. Let's say the Curry Family can cook, and I can fight. Now I can't cook worth a lick, but the Currys—boy, they can throw down in the kitchen! But they can't fight their way out of a wet paper bag. So then what we would do is establish a covenant. We would then say, "Whatever comes against you, I vow with my life that I'll protect and fight for you. So if they're attacking you, that means they're attacking me. And vice versa—when I'm hungry, you're going to feed me!"

This is the nature of all covenant relationships. Marriage? Same thing. When a husband and wife come together, the wife is responsible for bringing the supply she has to the marriage; the husband is responsible for bringing his supply to the marriage. He brings what she doesn't have, and she brings what he doesn't have. And that's what makes the marriage covenant work because there's a responsibility on both sides. If there is no responsibility or reciprocity, the relationship is dead.

So when God has a covenant with us, it is not merely mitigated to just a promise—you're supposed to do certain things on your side to walk in it. Abraham was faithful; therefore, he walked in a blessing with God, and he enjoyed the fullness of the blessing because he was faithful. He was not perfect! Abraham made plenty of mistakes. This is what people don't understand: You can be faithful and still mess up! But what you have to do is learn how to follow what God has instructed you to do. And when you make the things of God important to you, then you'll find that things begin to change because God is now able to move.

1 Samuel 2:35 gives us a definition of what "faithful" is:

> **And I will raise me up a faithful priest, THAT SHALL DO ACCORDING TO THAT WHICH IS IN MINE HEART AND IN MY MIND: and I will build him a sure house; and he shall walk before mine anointed for ever.**

According to this verse, the definition of "faithful" is to do a thing the way it's in God's heart and in God's mind. So then, *your* mind and *your* heart don't matter. In other words, unless your mind and your heart are bent to God's mind and His heart, you are not faithful. You can go to church every time the doors open, but do you go because you're looking for a girlfriend? Do you go because you're trying to better your job, or your career, or your business? Do you go because you're trying to find a husband? If you go because you are trying to do anything other than what church is designed for, you are not faithful. Most people think that *presence* is the same as *participation*. Presence is not the same as participation. Just because you showed up doesn't mean you truly showed up—you need to be where you're at. When you see two people sitting in a restaurant; husband and wife—you can always tell how long they've been married. They're both on their phones! They're *present,* but they didn't show up. If you value something, then you deal with it very preferentially. For me, things that I value, I treat better—because I value them! So while I may find some things less valuable than others, you will always be able to determine how weighty something is to me by how I handle it.

God says, *"I will raise me up a faithful priest,"* and He defines faithfulness as *"one who will do it the way that is in My heart and My mind."* I wouldn't do anything that's outside of the way God would want it done, because once you do a thing outside of the way God wants it done, you will find that it becomes subject to God's intervention. I wouldn't marry anybody outside of the way God said to do it. I wouldn't hang around people or have relationships outside of the way God said to do them. I would not spend money in a way that's against the way God said to do it, and I wouldn't give money in a way that's against what God said to do!

Some ministries and ministers constantly beg for money. You have to understand something: There should be a supply! Now, that doesn't mean you don't ask people to help, or you don't ask people to get involved. But when I see people in ministry who constantly beg for money, I realize God is warning me, "Be careful of trying to bankroll what God is trying to bankrupt." Because faithfulness is doing it the way that is in God's heart and God's mind, and the Bible says that a faithful man shall abound in blessings.

I'm not trying to pick on anybody, and I'm not trying to be mean, but if you're not abounding in blessings, the first place you'd better check is your faithfulness—your faithfulness to tithe, to give, to serve, to attend, to do the things that you know God has asked you to do and to do them in the way that is in God's heart and in His mind.

This is important; it's one of the things we're going to focus on in the next few chapters. If you get this, it will genuinely change everything, almost immediately, in your life.

> **1 SAMUEL 2:27**
> **And there came a man of God unto Eli, and said unto him, Thus saith the LORD, Did I plainly appear unto the house of thy father, when they were in Egypt in Pharaoh's house?**

When the first thing a man of God says to you is a question, that's usually not a good thing. God sent this person to speak to Eli, and the first thing he said was, basically, "Did you somehow misinterpret what I told y'all a long time ago?"

From that moment forward, it's downhill from there! God is like, "I showed up; I talked to you; I told you what I wanted; I gave the man of God a message for you; I spoke to your pastor to preach this to you; I sent this man *to your house!* And I appeared unto you, and I said, 'These are things I want.'"

When most of us hear the word "house," we think of a brick-and-mortar structure, a building. In this context, that is not what God means by "house." If you've ever heard of the house of David or the house of Saul, etc., you'll know a house is actually a system, a lineage, or a pedigree associated with that name. So when He said "I came to your house and was going to build you a house, and I allowed all the offerings to go to your house," He's saying "I made all that came into Israel come into your system, and I blessed your lineage; I blessed your pedigree, and I set you up to be a people unto Me who would walk in a blessing that you do not have enough room to contain, 'cause not only am I talking to you, but I am talking to your generations of descendants, to your children, to your children's children. I set up a house for you, and you have the nerve to honor your children above me!"

Because they were dishonorable, and because he was dishonorable, God said, "Your house will be affected. Your children will be affected, your children's children, all because of your lack of honor. Your whole house is now affected because of how you deal with God."

I think it's funny when I hear people tell their kids, "You've got to go to church," but then *the parent* won't. And they'll say, "Just do what I tell you to do." No, they're going to do what they *see you* doing. They're going to watch what's important to *you*. Now, I'm not saying there won't be times where things happen, and you have to do certain things, but let me tell you something—if, by and large, the football games, the basketball games, the baseball games the kids are in, if those are more important to you than church, then God will not be important to them.

My wife and I were talking to Pastor Barb about kids and sporting events, and whether they miss church, and this is what she said to us: "If it's a big event, then you want to go and support them." But she told us a story. She said when her kids were going through school, because of the area they lived in, the majority of the kids on the team were Christians. So when they tried to have practice on a church night, all the parents got together and said, "*No*. You can go ahead and have that practice, but nobody will be there!"

Here's the problem—*today*, because Christians are such a minority, we don't have that kind of leverage. She said her kids' coach moved practice to another night! This is the power of unity—when people stand for what's right! Stop teaching your kids to be dishonorable toward God, because they will honor what *you* honor. And if *you* make church important, if *you* make it weighty, if it's significant to *you,* they will fall in line. But if you are as lackadaisical as they are about it, stop talking about them, because they are a *reflection of you!* It's a fact. That's why He said, "Be it far from me."

Do you realize that the Bible says "God changes not"?

Did He just change his mind? *Yes, He did.*

He said, "I've told you that this is going to be one way, I made you a promise, but because of how you've handled Me... ."

I've heard people say "God promised me this, and I'm standing on the promises of God; I believe in the promises of God." Are the promises of God Yes and Amen? Of course, they are. Are the promises of God for you? Yes, they are. But if you're struggling, wondering why you're not walking in the promises, you should begin to reevaluate and ask, "Why is it far from me?"

He said, "You were going to walk before Me, but now, be it far from Me! Because whatever you honor, I honor. You honor Me, I'll honor you. And those that despise Me, I will despise." And then He gives a definition of what despising is—to "lightly esteem."

1 SAMUEL 2:31
Behold, the days come, that I will cut off thine arm, and the arm of thy father's house, that there shall not be an old man in thine house.

In Verse 31, God is saying, in other words, "I'm going to bless people *around* you, and *you* will struggle. You'll see other people prospering, and it'll be far from you."

When He said, "I'll cut off your arms," He didn't mean people would be walking around with no arms. The "arm" represents strength and power. So what He means is "I'm going to take away the strength, ability, and power that I put on you, on your family, on your children, your descendants. I will dial back the miraculous ability, the power, until everything in your house dies."

1 SAMUEL 2:33
And the man of thine, whom I shall not cut off from mine altar, shall be to consume thine eyes, and to grieve thine heart: and all the increase of thine house shall die in the flower of their age.

To paraphrase this verse, God is saying, "The faithful ones that I raise up, I'm going to raise them up, and you're going to have to go to them to eat. You're going to have to go work for them to get a piece of silver. You're going to have to serve those that are faithful in order for you to survive. You'll have to depend on the kindness of strangers."

I'm amazed by how they lost their inheritance—it affected not only their house, but also their children and their children's children missed out. It affected everything *concerning* them. Because they were irresponsible, it brought them to a place of being subject to the kindness of strangers, to the charity of other people.

God thinks honor is extremely important. I have to get you to understand this: HONOR IS SIGNIFICANT TO GOD. It is not something that is to be played with; it is not something that is easily dismissed, because God expects honor—and how you deal with things is how God deals with you. If you do not honor the things God expects you to do, if you "lightly esteem" them, then what?

MARK 6:1–6
And he went out from thence, and came into his own country; and his disciples follow him. And when the sabbath day was come, he began to teach in the synagogue: and many hearing him were astonished, saying, From whence hath this man these things? And what wisdom is this which is given unto him, that even such mighty works are wrought by his hands? Is this not the carpenter, the son of Mary, the brother of James, and Joses, and of Judas, and

Simon? And are not his sisters here with us? And they were offended at him. But Jesus said unto them, A prophet is not without honour, but in his own country, and among his own kin, and in his own house. And he could there do no mighty work, save that he laid his hands upon a few sick folk, and healed them. And he marveled because of their unbelief. And he went round about the villages, teaching.

It amazes me, in Verse 4, how Jesus said, *"A prophet is not without honor."* And in the Aramaic Bible, it says: *"There is no prophet that is DESPISED except in his city, among his kindred, and in his house."*

"Without honor" is translated as "despised."

Many people think dishonor is an act of intention. In other words, "I didn't do anything to you, so I'm not dishonorable," and that's not "dishonor." Dishonor is a lack of response, a lack of doing the right thing. Dishonor is a lack of applying the right amount of esteem and regard to a person, a situation. That's why Jesus says in Luke 20:25, *"Render unto Caesar that which belongs to Caesar."* To whom honor is due, give honor. To whom respect is due, give respect. One translation says, "If you owe a bill or owe a toll, pay it!" That's honorable! To not treat a debt or financial obligation as weighty means you don't intend to pay it. It's not important to you. And because you won't pay it, then you're being dishonorable toward the person to whom you are indebted.

Honor is a major issue today, particularly among young people. They have been bred into a culture of "Whatever!"

Their response to everything is "Whatever!"

And God's like, "No, no, it's not 'Whatever.'"

God expects you to honor those He has placed in your life—your leaders, your pastors, your bosses. Even when you don't like them! Because honor is not for them; it's for *you.*

And you can always tell the people who are dishonoring. Sometimes people will come to me at church and call me by my first name. They won't call me "Pastor." I don't care; I know what I am! I know who I am, and I'm confident in the calling God's given me. So you're not helping *me* by calling me Pastor; it's not reminding *me* of anything. It's reminding *you* because "Gene" can't do anything for you.

There's kind of a running joke, if you will, on the outside—places I visit—among people I know, ministers I know. They'll say something to me like "You know, you don't have to wear a suit when you come to preach for us, right?"

Okay, I don't preach in a suit for *you* in the first place. I'm well aware of what I have to do for you. But I don't do it for you. I do it because I honor the position and the office God has given me. So I don't show up in a Hawaiian shirt and khaki shorts. If that's what you do, knock yourself out! I'm not going to judge you for what you do. But I can tell you this much—Not Today! Because I believe in the call on my life from God, I believe in the office.

Listen, you can say what you want to about whether you like the president of the US, or don't like this president; whether you like the last president or the president before that. I don't really care what your opinions are of any of those individuals, because it doesn't matter to me. Here's what matters to me: You have never seen any of them deliver the State of Union Address in a Hawaiian shirt. None of 'em! So are you telling me they value their office? As I watched the State of

Union address recently, I found it funny how every time the president made some grandiose statement, people stood up and clapped and cheered—yet sometimes one side wouldn't respond at all. They were just mean-mug, and I was having flashbacks, thinking, "That's just like church! They're havin' church!"

I'm astounded how the world has a better understanding of honor than we Christians do. You can say what you want to about Catholicism as a whole, and I can tell you that I vehemently disagree with the majority of what happens in Catholicism. Not judging, I'm just at a different place personally. But I can tell you one thing: you can learn a lot from the Catholic church when it comes to honor and reverence. I don't understand why people don't see it. Notice that Jesus said, "A PROPHET IS NOT WITHOUT HONOR" or "A prophet is only DESPISED in his own town, among his own people, and in his own house." Anywhere else the prophet goes, he or she is regarded for holding the office of a prophet! But familiarity will cause you not to hear what's being said to you.

Listen, I never get familiar with my spiritual Father, never. He may come and stay in my house, and we may laugh, we may joke, we cut up a *lot*—anybody who's ever traveled with us will tell you, we cut up *pretty bad*. But I *never* lose sight of God's voice speaking through his voice. Never. There's no other voice, there's no other minister, no other preacher that will speak into my life more than he will. I won't allow it! You're not going to get so *familiar* to where you begin to not apply honor to what is coming from the one God has designed and designated to speak to your life. Because that's what God said! A pastor is not without honor except in his own church! A prophet is not without honor but in his own house. A husband is not without honor but in his own home.

Was Jesus mad because they wouldn't honor Him, so he just didn't do anything for them? He said he couldn't! Why couldn't he? Because they didn't put honor on Him. Let me say it to you in a very culturally identifiable and current way: They would not put any *respect* on His name. And because they wouldn't give respect to His name, there was nothing He could do.

I've watched people go through tough and challenging situations, and I have the answer they need—literally, straight from the Throne, *I have the answer*. But because they have no respect, they don't seek my counsel. If they had respect, they'd come to talk to me. If they had respect, they'd come to ask me for advice. But since they give no honor to my position as their pastor? They miss out on their opportunity. Because what can I do if I'm not invited in? See, "intruding" is going to a place where one should not be. And *INTRUDING* is one of the I's of Dishonor.

The nature of honor isn't doing something wrong to someone. Honor is respecting someone enough to do right by them. Some people say, "Well, I haven't done anything to disrespect you or dishonor you, I just haven't done anything. . . . " Well, okay, that's a problem. Because *to do nothing* is to dishonor them. Remember, to dishonor something is to *lightly esteem* it—to think it's light, to think it's no big deal, to think it's not significant. It's when you opt to sit and listen to a recording of a message your pastor preached that day—which they have gone straight before God, into the throne room, to get for you— rather than be present for the service because you thought it wasn't even worth showing up for.

You say, "Well, I haven't done anything to you!"

No, you just didn't show up.

That's why when a highly successful person shows up at a meeting, some people might say, "Oh, look! So-and-so has honored us with their presence!"

What word did they use?

Honor.

"So you mean to tell me that *a person showing up is honoring?*"

Yes.

Let's talk about INTRUDING.

PROVERBS 25:6
Put not forth thyself in the presence of the king, and stand not in the place of great men.

Notice what this verse tells you. Doesn't the Bible say that a man's gift makes room for him and brings him before great men?[1]

So what is this telling you?

Don't do it for yourself.

Some people want to put themselves in a place where they were not asked to be. They're intruding! And they don't know that it's dishonorable. You don't go into a place where you weren't invited to go! If somebody asks you to do something somewhere, you go within the confines of what they've asked you to do, and you stay there! Going beyond that is not taking the initiative, it's taking the liberty.

Initiative is taking into account what you were asked to do, and then executing within that context or framework.

Liberty is taking your own ideas and trying to force them into something somebody asked you to do.

Now all of a sudden when the project comes back to the person who invited your help, it's completely different because you had a better idea—it's intruding!

God says you don't put *yourself* there; you let the gift make room.

---

[1] Proverbs 18:16.

"Well, what if the gift ain't moving fast enough?"

Then your character isn't moving fast enough.

LUKE 14:7–11
And he put forth a parable to those which were bidden, when he marked how they chose out the chief rooms; saying unto them, When though art bidden of any man to a wedding, sit not down in the highest room; lest a more honorable man than thou be bidden of him; and he that bade thee and him come and say to thee, Give this man place; and thou begin with shame to take the lowest room. But when thou art bidden, go and sit down in the lowest room; that when he that bade thee cometh, he may say unto thee, Friend, go up higher: then shalt thou have worship in the presence of them that sit at meat with thee. For whoever exalteth himself shall be abased; and he that humbleth himself shall be exalted.

This parable says, to paraphrase, "When you show up, don't take the best seat! Because the problem is, you don't know how people see you! And if someone shows up who has more honor than you, then *you* gonna have to give up *yo* seat and do the walk of shame to the back of the room! But if you sit in the back of the room, and people call you forth, now you do the walk of honor—because everybody gets to watch how you have just been brought out of nothing into something."

Jesus is saying, "Let *God* elevate you into a place where you should be. Don't try to force *yourself* into a spot where you don't belong! 'Cause you'll start *intruding* into a place where you should not be! Now all of a sudden, you think everybody in the church should listen to *you* because *you* think you should preach—*you're* now the pastor, *you* now have a word for somebody—You don't have *anything*! Sit in the back of the room and wait for *God* to elevate you and bring you to a higher place when you are ready."

It is not easy to do the things that are necessary to be in ministry! People have *no idea* what it takes!

They have no clue. I was living in a house that was getting foreclosed on. And I was praying—*while I was having services* for the 30 people we had when we started the church—that someone would not show up to look for my car, a repo man would not come knocking on the door while I was trying to have service, that they wouldn't come to the door and throw us out. People have no clue what it's like!

When most people have a yard sale, they're cleaning their house. They're putting everything they *don't* want out so somebody can buy it.

I was putting things out I *did* want. And I sold them for next to nothing to get twenty, thirty dollars to go buy food. That I then took half of it to cook for people who came to our church service!

People have no idea what it costs. There's a price that has to be paid.

You see me now, and you're like, "Oh, Pastor's doing pretty good now!"

Yeah!

Lest we not forget the years of struggle, the years of working and having stuff turned off on me, while I was working in the house, trying to build a church. The water would get turned off; then I'd have to call the water company and work with them to get them to turn it back on again.

YOU LET GOD ELEVATE YOU. You let *God* bring you forth, you let *God* take you from the back to the front; that's where the honor is.

Putting yourself in a spot you weren't given is dishonorable. It's dishonorable for you to try to take a position you are not in. Because if you're not careful, you'll get to the Methuselah Theory. The Methuselah Theory is when you think, "Well, I've been around long enough that I'm important, that I'm this, and I'm that." You ain't.

They call it the Methuselah Theory because Methuselah was the oldest recorded person in the Bible. So people think, "Well, because I'm old, I have a certain right." You don't have anything. God is not governed by age, in chronological time. He's governed by revelation and truth. If you walk in revelation and truth, you will be exalted. When you're humble, God will bring you forward.

I am floored when I see people who are *rushing* to try to get to the pulpit. I am absolutely floored. You want to know why? God had to twist my arm to get me to do it. He really did. He had to threaten my life—you think I'm joking; I'm serious! I didn't want it, wasn't gonna do it! And I see people *rushing*—"I'm anointed; I'm the prophet of so-and-so; I'm this and that"—*seriously?* Do you have *any idea* what you're asking for?

It's intruding! It's intruding into places you are not supposed to be. And I'm telling you, every time you put yourself in a spot you shouldn't be, you are going to feel the crunch.

PROVERBS 26:17
He that passeth by, and meddleth with strife belonging not to him, is like one that taketh a dog by the ears.

The Bible talks about gossip—do you know what gossip is? Gossip is participating in listening to, or having conversations about, stuff that you are not able or in authority to fix, change, or affect. That's gossip.

"Well, I don't say anything, I just listen!" Still gossip. You're meddling in stuff that is not your affair. And the Bible says it's like grabbing a dog by the ears! *Intruding.* Can't mind your own business, can't stay where you're supposed to be. You know what you're supposed to do. Everybody wants to come talk to you and tell you about their problems. And you listen. And you become their garbage can.

Intruding!

Or here you are, you're representing people, you become the Johnnie Cochran[2] of the church world. So if they have a problem, now you have one too!

"I just don't like the way so-and-so is treated!" Okay, does that have anything to do with you?

So many people get caught up in stuff that has nothing to do with them, and they pick up offenses from other people because they're meddling in things they should not be involved with. If you're passing by, keep on passing by.

"Look, that has nothing to do with me, I'm sorry."

"Well, I just wanted to talk to you about—"

"Well, listen, you're talking to the wrong person. I don't wanna hear it."

"Well, you shoulda *heard* what Pastor said about you!"

"Well, until he says it to me? I don't wanna hear it from you."

I'm focused! Do you know what the difference is between a laser and a light bulb?

Focus. That's it!

Many people are so unfocused and so undisciplined that anytime a problem jumps up—anything that happens—they're always in the mix of it. As soon as I say, "Well, who was involved in that," certain names come up. I say, "*Really?* Why are you always in the middle of something?"

---

2 An American lawyer known for his advocacy for victims of police brutality.

Because you're a passerby who meddles in things that don't belong to you, and then you wonder why you're viewed as not honorable.

> **JOHN 21:18–22**
> **Verily, verily, I say unto thee, When thou wast young, thou girdedst thyself, and walkedst whither thou wouldest: but when thou shalt be old, thou shalt stretch forth thy hands, and another shall gird thee, and cary thee whither thou wouldest not. This spake he, signifying by what death he should glorify God. And when he had spoken this, he saith unto him, Follow me. Then Peter, turning about, seeth the disciple whom Jesus loved following; which also leaned on his breast at supper, and said, Lord, which is he that betrayeth thee? Peter seeing him saith to Jesus, Lord, and what shall this man do? Jesus saith unto him, If I will that he tarry till I come, what is that to thee? Follow thou me.**

This passage says, in other words, "When you were young, you went where you wanted to go. But I'm revealing to you right now that some things are gonna befall you, and someone else is gonna take you where you *don't* wanna go, and you're going to be stretched wide, and someone else is going to dress you.

Peter looked at John and said to Jesus, "What shall happen to him?"

The Bible says, *"Who am I to judge another man's servant[3]?"*

I don't look at what other people are called to do, I don't judge other people on their ministry and what they have to do, what God has asked them to do.

What does that have to do with me?

---

[3] Romans 14:4.

I don't care how so-and-so's church does it. How they think about things has nothing to do with me. I do not meddle in what does not belong to me.

Jesus did not explain to Peter what John's future was going to be.

It is none of your business to be worrying about what other people are doing, what other people are called to.

"How come this person gets to do this? Why can't I get to do this? Why am I not doing this? Why don't I have that?"

I don't know the exact reasons—sometimes I do, sometimes I don't! But the fact remains that when Peter asked, "You know that guy that says you love him? What's gonna happen to him?"

Jesus said, "If I make him live until I come back, what is it to you?"

Intruding.

Stepping into places where you should not be. Having conversations about stuff you should not have.

What business is it of yours what God is doing in someone else's life?

Gossipers.

So many people are so worried about somebody else that they forget to perfect themselves.

And listen, haters are the breakfast of champions! So if you don't have any haters, you ain't doing this thing right!

You have to be careful with the world of comparison. Because the moment you start looking at somebody else—"Well how come they have this? How come this is this? How come that is that?"—*You* will struggle. Because now you're intruding in a place where God didn't put you.

You know, Peter stayed getting checked!

That's why I love Peter. Peter reveals to you that you can be flawed and still make it. You can struggle with these things and still get it.

I don't get into what other people have or don't have, do or don't do, how they spend their money or how they don't spend their money. The church has some very critical people; it's amazing to me.

Intruding. Got an opinion about everything. You weren't invited, weren't asked.

"Oh, Pastor, by the way, while I've got you—"

I *hate* that!

I'll bring somebody in to my office. I'll have an issue I need to deal with, so I'll address it or ask them a question about something. They'll answer it, and I'll go, "Thank you so much," and they'll go, "Oh, Pastor, while I'm in here, while I've got your attention—"

You don't have my attention. I have *yours*!

Intruding.

"Well, you know, Pastor, it's none of my business, but I just wanted to share this with you."

You start out with, "It's none of my business, but—"

What I'd prefer you do is take out the "but" and put in a period!

You know how people do!

"Uhh, listen, I don't wanna gossip or nothin', but—"

Take out the "but," put a period on it, call it done. 'Cause I don't wanna hear it!

Some of you, you'll listen to stuff, and you think you're being a good Christian by just listening.

"All I was doing was listening!"

No, you're being dishonorable 'cause you're allowing somebody else to pull you into some garbage you shouldn't be hooked up into.

Can you all imagine how successful you could be if you could get some of these things and understand what you should not be mixed up in? I've seen more people derailed because they picked up the offense of somebody else—literally! They pick it up and carry it; they're like, "Oh, this is mine now, I'm gonna grind this ax. I feel bad for my fellow brother, and I'm just representing them." No, you're not. What you're doing is being nosy and meddling in places where you should not be.

I don't know about you, but I don't wanna grab dogs by the ears. That's just too close for comfort, that's too dangerous. It's ridiculous how people don't understand to not push themselves into a place where they should not be. And God is like "Why would you feel the need to intrude? If your gift will make room for you, then allow your gift to take you there!"

PROVERBS 18:16
A man's gift MAKETH room for him, and bringeth him before great men.

This verse says a man's gift *makes* room. That means there *was no room* for you. But if you have God's gift in you, it will *make* room for you. But you've got to allow whatever that process is to make it. It doesn't say "A man's gift *forces* room." It says it *makes* room for him.

The NIV (New International Version) puts it this way: *"A gift opens the way and ushers the giver into the presence of the great."*

We don't intrude. We allow the gift to make room. We allow it to usher us into greatness. And if you understand, you'll stay out of other people's nonsense.

I was going through some things about six or seven months ago, and I called my spiritual father, and he said to me "Son, be careful, because here is what's happening: if Satan can't get *you* into a battle, he's going to put people *around* you to try to pull you into one."

He was telling me if I were not careful, I would have allowed people to *intrude* and cause *me* to pick up the offense or pick up things that were not meant for me. I don't meddle in other people's things. If you don't want me in it, knock yourself out. But when it falls apart, remember, you didn't want me in it!

The Bible doesn't say to *counsel* the feeble-minded.

It says to comfort them.

You know what comfort is?

"Awww, poor baby, it's gonna be okay! It's all right. You're gonna be just fine!"

"Pastor, I need your help, I need some counsel, I need some help —"

"Awww, it's okay! God loves you, and so do I!"

You can't counsel feeble-minded people. When you tell them over and over again and they're just not listening, they're not getting it? Then I'm usually like, "You know what? Okay. All right! I'm done."

You want to know why?

Because people are sometimes on an assignment. And if you're not careful, you will think "Oh, I'm just being a good Christian by being a good ear." No, you are meddling in something that has nothing to do with you, and it's designed or sent to cause strife and problems and to derail the purpose and the plan of God for *your* life. You *comfort* the feeble-minded, you don't counsel. Otherwise, they will continuously intrude, and you have to talk about the same thing over and over and over again.

When I went through Bible college, I went through a biblical counseling class, and one of the first things I learned was "if you've got to keep talking about the same thing for more than three sessions, it's a wrap." That person is not trying to change. They just want a garbage can; they want to vent.

All of you know people like that! Y'all talking about the same thing this year that you fought about last year. You think, "I just wish they'd get it! If they could just get it—"

They're not going to get it. Stop casting pearls before swine and give focus to the things God has for you. Stop intruding into a place you weren't asked into. Because if you were genuinely asked into that place, they would say, "Okay, talk to me." They might have to come back a second time and go, "You know what, I tried what you told me to do, but I'm just not sure that I've got it right, so could you help me?" No problem. Let me counsel you. But if I have to keep telling you the same thing over and over and over again, "ain't nobody got time for that!" What that truly means is you haven't invited me in, and I'm intruding into a spot that you haven't given me the authority to deal in.

Dad Hagin told me a story about being with some ministers who were talking about this other minister who had to go through a divorce and was now remarried. In their denominational belief system, they believed he was not allowed to be divorced and then remarried. So they were having this conversation, and Dad Hagin said he was just standing there, listening to them. He returned to his room to pray—back then they had pull-chains on the lights. He pulled the chain to turn the light off and knelt down by the bed to pray. Well, the light came back on. So he immediately jumped up and pulled it again, and nothing changed; the light stayed on. He turned around—and Jesus was standing there!

Jesus looked at him and said, *"**Who are you** to judge another man's servant?"*

If that had been me, you would've had to change my drawers and everything else! I would've been like, "Hold up! I'm sorry, what did I do?"

Dad Hagin told Jesus, "I wasn't judging another man's servant."

Jesus said, "When you sat there and listened to them, and you didn't correct it, it's just as if you were saying it.

"He's *My* servant. Not yours. If I have a problem with it, *I'll* deal with him about it. I can make him stand, and I can make him fall.

"But who are you?"

Somebody came to me one time who believed they were a prophet; they just thought they knew everything concerning the things of God, and wouldn't sit still. I tried to help them; I even brought some of the elders of the church in with me to try to help this person because they just weren't hearing what I was saying. So I literally started going through Matthew 18 line by line, confronting them about things that they were doing and thinking wrong. This person had come into my office and said, "Pastor, I need to meet with you."

And I said, "Okay."

And they said, "Pastor, how come you let So-and-so be a head of a ministry?"

And I said, *"Excuse me?"*

"Well, So-and-so, I just don't think they're right with God."

I don't think *you're* right with God!

Who are you to judge another man's servant? Even if they have made mistakes! What if they're in restoration? We're not gonna give up the call of God because somebody's made a mistake! We're going on with the things of God! We're going on forward with God. We're gonna make adjustments and keep moving! Now, if you've got proof of something they are currently doing *right now,* let's talk about that. But if you're going to bring up their past, Satan, you're intruding! You are stepping into a place you don't belong, and more importantly, what you are telling me is you don't trust my judgment. And now we've *really* got a problem. I told them to check their love walk. Criticizing other people and how they serve God—check your love walk!

Elijah came before God and said, "God, I'm the only one who loves you, I'm the only one who serves you. You don't understand, God, *nobody* wants to serve you like I do!"

God was like, "You know what, dude, *for real*? I've got a *whole gang* of folks that haven't bent the knee to Satan. So you are *not.*"

CHAPTER 2
INFERIOR

One of the things I've noticed here lately is, we have been bringing a lot of light. And with that comes an attack. While many of us are experiencing different types of symptoms in our physical body, God is our healer. And just because you're under attack doesn't mean you'll stay under attack! We have been bringing a *lot* of light—and I want you to understand that this subject of honor is significant. The more I delve into it, the more I'm convinced this is the reason why people struggle. It really is! Because God is a God of honor. And God is definitely honorable, and He expects us to be honorable.

Let's recap some of what we already covered.

1 SAMUEL 2:29–30
Wherefore kick ye at my sacrifice and at mine offering, which I have commanded in my habitation; and honourest thy sons above me, to make yourselves fat with the chiefest of all the offerings of Israel my people? Wherefore the LORD God of Israel saith, I said indeed that thy house, and the house of thy father, should walk before me for ever: but now the LORD saith, Be it far from me; for them that honour me I will honour, and they that despise me shall be lightly esteemed.

In the above passage, God is saying, "If you don't take Me seriously, I don't take you seriously."

1 SAMUEL 2:35
And I will raise me up a faithful priest, that shall do according to that which is in mine heart and in my mind: and I will build him a sure house; and he shall walk before mine anointed for ever.

God had said this priest's family would stand before Him, and his house would stay before Him forever. But because of how they handled the things of God—notice he said, "You honored your sons before Me. You've regarded the things your children were doing over what I told you to do, and you've let them run rampant, you've let them do whatever they wanted to do, and you've disregarded what *I've* told you to do. So now your whole house will be affected."

It's tragic to think that God would allow this man's *entire house*, his entire system, his entire family, his entire lineage to have to beg for a piece of bread because of *his* dishonorableness.

Too many people fail to realize that one of the *main reasons* they struggle is that they are extremely dishonorable toward the things of God. They *lightly esteem* God; therefore, God lightly esteems them. Because He said, "those who honor me, I will honor."

What does "honor" mean?

Honor means to prefer something or someone; to put them above other situations. Having honor means that while everyone else is going through problems, you'll have answers to your problems.

See, that's the difference!

People think that if they honor God, they'll never have problems. Of course, that's not going to happen.

Everybody is going to have troubles, trials, and tribulations. And they'll have to go through some situations, too. The difference between those that are honorable toward God and those that aren't is that answers come. Help comes. Because God said, "I'll honor you because you honor Me."

So this man's dishonor affected his prosperity, his family's inheritance, his children, their children, and so on . . . and on . . . and on—

Over my years as a pastor, I've seen how when parents get in line — and I mean *both* parents—all of a sudden, their children get in line. And if there's only one parent—a single mother or single father— when *that* parent gets in line, it's almost like something *pulls* the children right into line. We need to understand how we can affect future generations by how *we* handle honor. And honestly—I'm going get up on this soapbox here—young kids today have no understanding of honor.

The first authority figure children meet is their parents. And if parents don't handle that position of honor properly, when those kids go to school and meet their teachers, they'll give them no honor. When they run into the police, they'll get no honor. And I'm telling you, there are institutions *full* of people who don't know how to honor. The body of Christ ought not to be that way—we know better. We know better, so we're supposed to *do* better.

So here is God, making it clear that honor is affecting this people's prosperity.

What else does honor mean?

To give honor means to make someone or something important, to make it weighty, to make it significant, to put a value on it. If a man honors his wife, or a wife honors her husband, she puts a high value on him, and he puts a high value on her. She's not insignificant, and he's not insignificant—there's honor present! And when honor is present, you make it weighty. You make it heavy; you make it significant.

Sometimes I hear a husband say things like, "Well, my boys called, and they wanted to go out, and the wife is upset about it." I want to ask, "At what point did your boys give birth to your children? When are your boys lying in bed keeping you warm at night?"

…And if they are, that's a problem! That's a whole different message!

Honor gives things value. Honor makes them weighty, and honor makes them significant.

Some people will do a terrible job at work, and then want to be promoted. They want to run things, and they can't manage what they're already doing! Have you ever heard of the Peter Principle? It's what happens in companies and organizations when no one can get a certain person to perform in their job. So what do they do? Promote 'em.

Think about your boss—unless your boss is me! Whenever you wonder, "How did such an inept person get in charge?" It's the Peter Principle. If they can't do the job, promote 'em.

God doesn't work that way. God expects faithfulness, and God expects honor.

Have you ever noticed how people can't stay focused? I've been studying a lot lately, and I'm learning something about focus. Focus is so important.

Remember the difference between a light bulb and a laser? It's *focus*.

A laser is a focused beam of amplified light; you can cut through steel with a laser. I don't care how much steel you put up against a light bulb. It's not cutting through anything!

When you consider something weighty or valuable, *you focus on it because it's important to you.* So when you serve God—I don't care if you're in Sunday school with the kids, or on the praise-and-worship team, or in the sound booth; I don't care if you're cleaning the bathrooms! Considering your service important enough to do it with excellence is *everything.* If you've got it in your head that one position is lower than another, you are not reading the Bible! Because the Bible is very clear that the reward *I* get is the same reward *you* get, no matter where in the body of Christ you serve.

Some people grumble, "If I could be honest, that's unfair to me! Why do I have to work so hard and do so much, and you still get the same reward I get?" That should tell you how important God thinks even the little things are.

Could you imagine if Noah built the ark and God hadn't given him instructions on how do it?

Could you imagine if Noah said, "Okay. You want it to be *this* big, but I'm going to build about a 15-footer because I can get that done quicker"?

Can you imagine the look on his face when two elephants showed up?

God is very precise; God is very specific; and God is very much into the details. So when you think of these things, honor can cost you *a lot*. Dismissively dealing with God can cost you *a lot*.

So our next "I" is INFERIOR.

PROVERBS 3:9–10
"Honour the LORD with thy substance, and with the firstfruits of all thine increase. So shall thy barns be filled with plenty, and thy presses shall burst out with new wine."

Two things are addressed in Proverbs 3:9-10. The first thing is your bank account.

I have a barn. A barn is where you store things. I've got a few of them! And I put money into them on a regular basis. My barn happens to be at Wells Fargo—all of them!

He says, *"Your presses will burst with new wine."* Now listen, I don't know about you, but old wine is not the same as new wine. New wine is wine you didn't have—or let me say it this way: it's business you didn't have! But He puts a prerequisite on it.

As a kid, I learned how to program computers using BASIC, a language in the computer world. They hardly use it anymore, but back in those days, you would type in commands like "If ___, Then Go To ___." In other words, "If something exists *this* way, then go to *that*."

So if you put into the programming that when you type the number 1, the computer takes you to a particular game, then if you type 2, 3, 4, 5, or 6, or 10, or any number other than 1, nothing happens because it's waiting for the proper command! "If *this* exists, then go to *that*."

Our scripture passage says, *"Honor the Lord WITH THY SUBSTANCE and WITH THE FIRSTFRUITS OF THY INCREASE."* He says if you do that, so shall your barns—or bank accounts—be filled with plenty, and your presses shall burst with new wine.

Let's go back and look at it again:

"Honor the Lord with thy SUBSTANCE." Substance is what you already have—your bank account.

Then it refers to *"the firstfruits of thy INCREASE."* Increase is the new wine that comes out of the press.

Do you truly honor God in the area of your finances? Or do you struggle with giving a tithe?

I love teaching these types of messages after the offering has been received. Do you know why?

You can't go back and change it! And you can't say, "Pastor's preaching money outta my pocket!"

Because I don't know what *you're* going to do, but *I* am going to honor the Lord with not only my substance—which is what I currently have—but I'm also going to honor him with the first fruits of the increase that comes to my life. And notice He says *FIRST* fruits!

So many people get stuck on the money, and they forget about the fact that it's the *first part* that He wants. Because if you give Him the first parts, everything behind it is blessed. See, God is a God of order. That's why Elijah told the widow, "Make me a cake first, and then go ahead and do what you said you were gonna do." If she hadn't made his first, this would've been a problem!

God is a God of order and priority because the priority is an indication of your heart. Plain and simple.

Whatever's important to you, you will put first in your life. That's why when God was dealing with Eli, He said "You know what? You honored your sons before Me."

What was Eli dealing with? *What was first* in his life?

God said, "You put them first!"

Is God really first in your life?

I love how people will say, "I put God first," and then you won't see them anywhere near a church!

31

I wonder, how did you come up with "God first" when God really *isn't*?

They'll put their jobs first—"Well, you know, I've got a schedule, and I've got things I've gotta do, so church comes second."

Well, then, what did you honor first? When you need healing, go ask your job to heal you. When you need deliverance, go ask your job to deliver you.

To honor God is to put Him first.

You need to deal with godly things *first*.

One of the first things I do in marriage counseling is ensure that both parties—husband and wife, or future husband and future wife—are going to put God's Word first. If they're not going to put God first, there's no point in having any further discussions, because I'm not a counselor. Now, if you want to be in counseling for the next *six years,* you'd better be writing some checks! I don't mind buying myself a new boat off of your counseling fees! But otherwise, if we want to get this done quickly, then we go to the Word of God. One word from God can change everything! So for me, the Word is always the basis—it's called The Triangle. The man is in one corner of the base, the woman is in the other, and God is at the top. As they move toward God, they get closer to each other. If you want to see a marriage go off the rails, it's when a wife is chasing God, or a husband is chasing God, and the other spouse isn't. The marriage will fly off the rails in a New York second. But when they're chasing God *together*, when they're growing together? *Nothing* can break that because their priority is God.

> **LUKE 12:31–32**
> **"But rather seek ye the kingdom of God; and all these things shall be added unto you. FEAR NOT, little flock; for it is your Father's good pleasure to give you the kingdom.**

Notice the order in these verses. The first thing He says is, "If you're going to seek the kingdom of God *first*, FEAR NOT." Do you want to know why? Because the first thing that will creep into your life is fear.

Fear that you won't make it, fear that you won't have enough. Here are the disciples in the back of the boat, and Jesus says, "We're going to the other side." They wake him up, and the first thing they ask him is, "Do you care that we die?"

Fear will cause you to question God's care for you—that's why He said: *"FEAR NOT, for it is your Father's good pleasure to give you the Kingdom."*

> **LUKE 12:33–34**
> **Sell that ye have, and give alms; provide yourselves bags which wax not old, a treasure in the heavens that faileth not, where no thief approacheth, neither moth corrupteth. For where your treasures is, there will your heart be also.**

In other words, *"Take your worldly stuff—sell it, and take care of other people with it. Then you'll have a money bag that nobody can take from you."*

The NIV (New International Version) reads: *"Sell your possessions and give to the poor. Provide purses for yourselves that will not wear out."*

Purses! Wallets! What do you keep in your wallet? Stuff *you need —money, ID, credit cards*. He said, "If you hold on to *your* stuff, then I can't give you a supply that doesn't run out. But if you learn how to be a conduit, I'll give you a source of wealth that doesn't run out—a treasure that is not just natural; it's *eternal*." Wherever you put your money, that's really where your heart is. So when you've got house payments, and you don't tithe? You're letting God know, "My heart's in my house." Now listen to me—*God is obligated to destroy all idols.*

So when you're losing it all, it's because you won't put God first. It's a problem of where your heart is. Because if your heart were with God, He'd always come first! But fear will cause you to allow your heart to follow things it shouldn't.

Do you realize there are 38 parables in the Gospels? Thirty-eight parables—and almost *half* of them are about money and possessions. Did you know that *one out of every ten verses* in the Gospels deal with the subject of money? The entire Bible offers 500 verses on prayer, 500 verses on faith, and more than *2,000 verses on money and possessions.* Yet most pastors are afraid to talk about money because they don't want to offend people.

I know that God will bring more—I don't trust in man; I don't trust in chariots; I don't trust in horses; I shall remember the name of the Lord.

God is God.

And when you get into fear, it will cause you to not put God first. You'll put everything else first!

LUKE 16:10
He that is faithful in that which is least is faithful also in much: and he that is unjust in the least is unjust also in much.

Listen, if I give you a little thing to do, and you think it's beneath you because it's small—maybe it's cleaning the bathrooms, maybe it's working as a greeter, maybe it's working in the sound booth—and you think it's small? If you can't be faithful to the little stuff? Jesus said this *Himself,* so it's not subject to debate: If you can't be faithful to the little thing that I asked you to do, then you are not faithful in the big stuff.

It's simple. He said, "Those that are faithful in the least are faithful also in much." Why? Because as little as it may seem, you still give it value and you still give it weight, and you handle it the way it's supposed to be handled.

LUKE 16:11
If therefore ye have not been faithful in the unrighteous mammon, who will commit to your trust the true riches?"

He's telling us that *"unrighteous mammon"* is money. If you can't even be trusted to handle *money*? Money is the *lowest* level of faithfulness. He said, "If you can't handle money, who will trust you with True Riches?" I have to get you to see that. Because so many people say things like "Well, if I had more, if I hit the lottery, I would give more." No, you won't! If you can't give ten cents off a dollar, you are not going to give ten percent off a million!

CNBC News reported that nearly *70 percent of lottery winners* go broke in three to five years.[4] Do you want to know why? Because their *soul* has not prospered. If you are poverty-minded, you will be *rich* and still be poverty-minded. Money doesn't change the person! The person has to know how to handle and steward what God has given them. And when people say, "Y'know, Pastor, if I had it I'd give it," I say, you wouldn't give it if there were three guys behind you with bazookas and a Rottweiler! You're airtight like a frog's behind, talking about what you're *going* to do.

Listen! He said, "If you can't handle *unrighteous mammon*, if you can't even deal with *money*, how are you going to deal with the things of God?" If money's got your life, how are you going to follow God? If money grips your fears, how will you follow God? If money keeps you from giving, from serving, from doing; if you take a job because it's about the money; if you take stuff because it's about the money; *if that's all that it is, how could you ever serve God?*

---

[4] Abigail Hess, "Here's Why Lottery Winners Go Broke," *CNBC*, CNBC, 25 Aug. 2017.

Everything God asked me to do—I may not have had a *nickel* to do it, but He called me to do it—He equipped me to do it!

But if *money* is your thing?

I've seen so many people take jobs that weren't in the best interest of their family, and say, "It's not about the money." Sure it is!

Don't pretend to be spiritual with me, sure it is

LUKE 16:13
No servant can serve two masters: for either he will hate the one, and love the other; or else he will hold to the one, and despise the other. YE CANNOT SERVE GOD AND MAMMON."

You cannot serve God and money. You just can't do it, because God will put you at odds with money.

Hoarding is a manifestation of the love of money. When people can't seem to let go of stuff—they've got the same pen they used in 1962—that's poverty-minded, that's the spirit of poverty! Don't you know pen technology has changed since 1962? Now listen, if it's a Mont Blanc or a Cartier pen or something like that, I understand that—but a *BIC*? Dear God, I'll buy you a whole new box of them!

See, people don't realize that a love of money will keep them from giving. It's not just about *chasing* money; it's about *hoarding* money. *Wherever your heart is, that's where your treasure is; and wherever your treasure is, that's exactly where your heart goes.* This is why you have to be careful—because wherever you put your money or whatever you put money into, that's where we know your heart is.

If you've ever purchased a house, you know the sellers want your bank statements! They could ask for your deposit records and figure out how much you've got in the bank—they don't want that! They want to look at your bank statements because they want to see where your money goes.

They want to know if you go to the Nasty Kitty every Friday night!

They want to know what you do with your money because your bank account and your credit report will reveal *your character*.

That's why when you try to buy a house, the mortgage lenders pull your credit report. They want to know how many houses or apartments you've run out on—because if you don't value your home, they want to know. They send a request to your previous landlords. They want to know how you handled paying them! They want to know if you've paid them on time because if you don't value the house you live in, the current roof over your head, they figure, "If you've got no honor for that, when push comes to shove, you ain't gonna pay what you owe me!"

That's why they look at those things. They want to see who you are.

And you know what's funny to me? Most Christians struggle in these areas. We should be the most prosperous people—if the Bible says we shouldn't be the borrower but the lender, why are Christians struggling like this?

MALACHI 1:1-8
The burden of the word of the LORD to Israel by Malachi. I have loved you, saith the LORD. Yet ye say, Wherein hast thou loved us? Was not Esau Jacob's brother? Saith the LORD: yet I loved Jacob, And I hated Esau, and laid his mountains and his heritage waste for the dragons of the wilderness. Whereas Edom saith, We are impoverished, but we will return and build the desolate places; thus saith the LORD of hosts, They shall build, but I will throw down; and they shall call them, The border of wickedness, and, The people against whom the LORD hath indignation for ever. And your eyes

shall see, and ye shall say, The LORD will be magnified from the border of Israel. A son honoureth his father, and a servant his master: if then I be a father, where is mine honor? And if I be a master, where is my fear? Saith the LORD of hosts unto you, O priests, that despise my name. And ye say, Wherein have we despised thy name? Ye offer polluted bread upon mine altar; and ye say, Wherein have we polluted thee? In that ye say, The table of the LORD is contemptible. And if ye offer the blind for sacrifice, is it not evil? And if ye offer the lame and sick, is it not evil? Offer it now unto thy governor; will he be pleased with thee, or accept thy person? saith the LORD of hosts.

They were bringing lame and sick animals—they were picking out the best, and they were sacrificing the worst.

They were sacrificing what they were going to lose anyway.

They were giving what didn't matter.

They were dealing with everything else that was important, and then whatever they had leftover, that's what they gave to God. And He said "If you did that to a governor, to a president, to a king, to a mere man—if you handled your governor that way, would he accept you? No—but yet you do that to Me."

MALACHI 1:13-14
Ye said also, Behold, what a weariness is it! And ye have snuffed at it, saith the LORD of hosts; and ye brought that which was torn, and the lame, and the sick; thus ye brought an offering: should I accept this of your hand? saith the LORD. But cursed be the deceiver, which hath in his flock a male, and voweth, and sacrificeth unto the LORD a corrupt thing: for I am a great King, saith the LORD of hosts, and my name is dreadful among the heathen.

He says, "Cursed be the person who has something better, but won't give the better thing."

That's what made it polluted and corruptible!

He said, "You have better, but you won't give better! Which means it's a sign of a lack of honor. That's why I believe you despise My name."

When I gave things to my pastor, I never bought something new for myself and then gave my pastor the old stuff. People do stuff like that all the time. They'll get a new 180-inch TV, and then they'll want to give the church their old floor-model box TV.

There was a story about Butterball—you know, the turkey?

Butterball has a 24-hour line you can call if you run into a problem with your turkey.[5] So this lady called and said, "I have this turkey that's been in my freezer for *ten years*—can I still eat it?"

Their representative told her, "I don't think you should." True story!

She said, "Okay, well, I'll just give it to the church."

People think like this! People function like this!

I *never* did that. If I bought myself something new, I'd buy the same thing for my pastor. I thought if I wanted to bless him, I wouldn't cheapen the blessing by handing him something I consider *inferior*.

I didn't bring the church an offering that was inferior.

That's what God is dealing with here in Malachi! He says, "You have better, but you don't have any honor because you think it's okay to bring little or nothing; you think it's fine not to tithe; you think it's

---

[5] "Turkey Talk Line," *Butterball*, www.butterball.com/about-us/turkey-talk-line

okay not to bring a supply; you think it's fine not to serve; you think it's all okay, and you have better!"

You'll go to your job and work your fingers to the nub for *them*, but you won't come to the house of God and do your part when you have better! He said how you deal with things is a sign of honor!

It's a sign of honor, how you deal with God.

Let me prove it to you, 'cause I can tell you this much—you'll lose what you don't honor. If you don't honor it, you'll lose it, and when you honor it, you'll qualify for more. And this is why so many people don't *have* more.

I'm going to pick on my wife for just a moment. A long time ago, she acquired a car. It was an older car, and when she first got it, she said, "Let me show it to you, Pastor!"

So I went outside and saw the car, and she said, "It's not much."

And I said "Hold on—stop speaking that! If you got blessed with it, if God gave you the money to get it—however it came to you—if God moved, then you treat that thing like it's a Porsche 911! Because what you honor will qualify you for more."

Listen, if you can't keep the house you have clean—I'm getting in your business right about now! If you're complaining about not having a landscaper to take care of the yard, complaining about not having a pool, if you're complaining about all that stuff and you can't seem to keep your house clean, stop asking for a bigger one! Bigger houses have more dust. Bigger houses have more yard. If you're believing God for more than one house and you're complaining about what it costs to take care of one? It's dishonorable! When you walk into whatever place you have—whether it's an apartment or a house—when you walk in, you say, "Thank You, God, for this house! I thank

You for all that You're doing in my life!" When you honor what you have, you qualify for more!

Quit asking for more if you can't be honorable with what you already have.

This is why it bothers me when my car gets dusty. I always joke and say, "Mercedes is gonna call and say, 'We're gonna come pick that up because you ain't treating it right!'" Listen to me; you'd better honor what you have!

If you want more, you have to be honorable toward what you already have.

Brother Keith told me this story. He was at a conference, and he was coming out of the hotel, and a lady walked up to him and said, "Brother Keith! You know, I just wanted to tell you that I so appreciate your ministry. I haven't given a *dime* to your ministry, but you guys have sent me so much material—you've just been such a blessing to me."

Brother Keith said, "Oh, that's okay, Ma'am! That's wonderful, and we're glad we can just be a blessing to you." He was trying to be courteous and cordial and nice, right?

As he was walking away, God checked him and said, "Don't you ever do that again. You're misrepresenting me."

Brother Keith said, "What do you mean I'm 'misrepresenting' You? I'm not misrepresenting You!"

God said, "Yes, you are! It's not *reaping and sowing*, it's *sowing and reaping*."

Let's look at our next scripture.

LUKE 21:1–4
And he looked up, and saw the rich men casting

their gifts into the treasury. And he saw also a certain poor widow casting in thither two mites. And he said, Of a truth I say unto you, that this poor widow hath cast in more than they all: For all these have of their abundance cast in unto the offerings of God; But she of her penury hath cast in all the living that she had.

First of all, what was Jesus doing watching the offering?

He was watching their hearts. He can tell where your heart is.

And he said, "She gave more than they did!"

What does that tell you? It's not about money. It's not about the amount.

So this is what God told Brother Keith. He said, "You know what? If the poor widow woman could give two pennies, that woman you spoke with could have given something."

This is why when people want to get close to me, but they don't want to do anything to serve the church?

"I want to hang out with Pastor!"

No, you don't do anything! You don't invest, you don't give, you don't serve, but you want to get close to me. And I give, and I serve, and I pay a cost. But you don't want to pay the cost; you want to get something for nothing.

I will not misrepresent God.

I've worked too hard to get the anointing I walk in, it took too much—you have *no idea,* the things I had to sacrifice and give to walk where I am, it doesn't come easy! And don't misrepresent God by thinking it does.

God said, "Even she could give two pennies."

There is no excuse for doing nothing. See, people think that dishonor is when someone says something about you or does something to hurt you. *Doing nothing is dishonorable.* Or, let me rephrase that—not doing something to the measure that you could.

This is where honor begins to count things as weighty and significant.

God cares about what you give. He doesn't want your *inferior* stuff. He doesn't want you to give more of yourself to a job, but then come to church and be *inferior* in your service to Him. He doesn't want that stuff. It's disrespectful, and it's dishonorable! Now, I'm gonna work hard for people who pay me, but I will *never* work harder for *anybody*, I will never have a level of excellence for *anybody* more than I would for God. And let me tell you something: Excellence is hard! If you're not careful, excellence will attract the hungry, and it'll agitate the incompetent. When you start holding the bar of excellence, people will start criticizing your efforts. "Well, I don't see why that matters." Because it *does*.

It matters because it does. When we have food out on the table at church, that matters. I tell you what, if I ever see someone cutting a donut into four pieces? I'm gonna lay hands on ya, get that spirit of poverty off of you! Because we are not impoverished people; we are to be a blessing, to be bountiful and abundant. We represent *God*, y'all. This is what we are supposed to be! Things should be top-notch, top shelf! When people see us do something, they should be like, "Wow!" We're not inferior, not second-class! When the bathrooms are cleaned, it should smell great in there, look great in there. People should not go in there and be offended, like, "What in the *world* happened in here? Who *died*?" They should go into our bathrooms and say, "Wow!"

This is honorable.

It matters how things look. *It matters* how clean things are. *It matters* to God.

We cannot present Him with inferior things.

It matters what kind of offering you bring.

One time years ago, I was teaching on finances in a Bible college. After class, a lady walked up to me and said, "Pastor Gene, I need to talk to you."

I knew it was coming, so I said, "Okay, what's up?"

She goes, "I can't give ten percent—I ain't doing it! I *might* be able to do three percent. You think I can get by with three percent?"

She happened to be in real estate. And I knew that, right?

So I said to her, "You ever sell a house where the commission is three percent?"

She said, "Yeah!"

And I said, "Would you take two percent instead?"

"*Absolutely not!*"

I said, "Would you take one and a half?"

"Not if it was supposed to be three!"

"Well then, you have your answer, don't you?"

Listen, y'all, the tithe is not the ceiling. The tithe is actually the *floor*. If you can't be trusted with *money*—unrighteous mammon— why would God trust you with the true riches? Why would God bless you if you can't handle the stuff you have now? If you make $25,000, $30,000, two dollars? Whatever it is that you make—if you can't be trusted to handle *that* well?

Your job constantly pulls you away from church. You say, "I've gotta get my life together." That's *your* problem.

And then you're on Facebook saying, "The struggle is real."

God said His yoke is easy, and His burden is light. When you honor God, He honors you. He takes care of you when you take care of Him. I watch people go from calamity to calamity to calamity to calamity. And it's because they're just not honorable! They'll promise you one thing then bring you stuff that's inferior.

In the 1970s, there was a TV show called *Good Times*. In one episode a neighbor lady wants to thank the Evans family by cooking them some meatloaf, and they find out she's been eating pet food! So when she arrives with this meatloaf, they're all looking at this thing suspiciously. Then they start to pray over it, and their son J.J. says, "The Lord is my German Shepherd!" Long story short, she realizes something's up, so they kind of confess to her what the problem is, and this is her response: "I eat pet food for me because I can't make ends meet. But do you really think so low of me to think that I would come to your house and bring you pet food?"

I might have to do a lot of things for *my* house, but when it comes to *God's* house? There were times when I was paying bills to take care of *God's* house, while *my* services were getting turned off.

See, how you deal with the things of God will determine your outcome. And if you're not honorable, if you're bringing what's inferior, what's second-rate, your leftovers—if you say, "I worked hard all day, so now I'm just gonna come here and help them do this, and I'm tired and I don't have any energy, I'm lethargic, but y'know, I'm here to *serve the Lord*"—well, if you can't bring your best, it's inferior.

God wants your best!

You want His best!

See, when we look at things through a different lens, you have to think about how God sees things. God blessed you with whatever it is you have. You may say, "Well, I don't have much." Whatever you have, God blessed you with it.

There's a thermostat on a wall in our church building. It's not a working thermostat; it just tells the temperature in the room. It does not control the air conditioning.

Now, listen to me. There's one unit in the building that is strictly a thermometer. There are two ones that are thermostats. The difference between a thermometer and a thermostat is a *thermometer* tells you what is going on in the room. The *thermostat* dictates what is *going* to happen in the room. If I turn the thermostat to 80 degrees, the temperature in the room goes to 80 degrees. If I turn it down to 60, the room goes to 60.

Are you a *thermometer*?

Or are you a *thermostat*?

Because either you are going to *set* the temperature, or you're going to be constantly reacting to it.

It's up to you. But when you live a life of honor, you're *honorable*.

On our Sabbath, we were out at the pool at the country club—we have a pool in our back yard, but here's what I believe: if the country club is gonna heat theirs, then I shouldn't have to heat mine!

So we met this gentleman at the country club, and we got to talking and he told us about his business and stuff. He has a business we might be able to use from time to time, so I told him I would reach out to him. He gave me his email address, and one of the first things I did was send him an email because I told him I would. It said, "Pleasure to meet you, just wanted to make an official introduction. Here's my email, my contact information, it was good to meet you, hopefully we'll see you out there again soon." *Because I said I would!*

As a Christian, you represent God by how you handle things. And if you want to represent God as "poor and can't keep his word," you're misrepresenting Him. And then you wonder why He's trying to bankrupt what you're trying to bankroll! If you have no supply for what you're doing, you might want to check how you're doing it, because God's not going to finance your disobedience. God's not going to give you the boat you want so you can be out on the water on Sunday when you should be in church. God's not going to give you a job ("Thank God for this job!") if the job is taking you away from church. And you're blindly unaware, thinking "This is God! God understands my heart." He *does* understand your heart! Because you show it.

Honor is such a big thing. You've *got* to teach your children honor. I mean, when I was a kid, we addressed people as "No, Sir," "Yes, Sir." It was "Mister This" or "Mister That." I don't know *what* has happened. I just don't understand. And people say, "Well, that was old school." Listen, some things that are old school are time-tested! And honor is not old school; honor is important! Because when you teach your children to be honorable, when you yourself are honorable, that sends a message: We are believers. We don't function the way the world functions! We're believers, the best of the best, the crème de la crème. We are the ones who are "called out," the *ecclesia*!

In Spanish, the word for "church" is *Iglesia*.[6] It comes from *ecclesia*[7] (or *ekklisía*), the Greek word for "church." So wherever you see the word "church" in the Bible, it is the Greek word *ecclesia*.

---

[6] "Iglesia = Church, Feminine Noun," Spanish to English Translation I Spanish Central, www.spanishcentral.com/translate/iglesia.

[7] "Ecclesia," *Merriam-Webster*, Merriam-Webster, www.merriam-webster.com/dictionary/ecclesia.

"*Ec*" means "out of."

"*Clesia*" means "called."

The church is "the called-out ones."

In biblical times, the ecclesia would pull together the key, prominent business leaders, the best of the best—the best warriors, the best fighters—and hold court with them regarding "how to go to war." *That's* the ecclesia.

You are the best of the best! You have been pulled out from the world for such a time as this—that's what the ecclesia was in the early church! It was the *best* fighters, the *best* business people, the *smartest* thinkers. They all came together in a room and discussed, "How do we go to war now?" That's why Jesus said, "The gates of hell shall not prevail against *My* ecclesia, *My* Called-Out Ones, the ones that I put *My* stamp on." You have no idea!

You thought when you walked into church some time ago that it was just another place where you were gonna show up, and God had a *whole different plan* for you. You are the Called-Out Ones! Nobody in His body is inferior; nobody in His body is not gifted; nobody in His body doesn't have a calling on their life; nobody in His body is not blessed; nobody in His body is not considered the best of the best!

God called you out. He called you out from the world—*why*? So you can be the best; you keep your word; you handle yourself with integrity and character so that when people see you, they're like, "I want what they've got!" And that's when you can say, "I know a Man."

This is what it's all about! But when people of the church are just as dishonorable as people of the *world*? It ought not be so. We ought to be the most honorable people on the planet. When people look at us, they ought to be like, "Wow—you can say what you want, but they're honorable."

Even if you've got a Hooptie,[8] you drive that thing like it's a Mercedes Benz.

If you don't have a car and you've got a bike? Drive that thing like it's a Bentley.

I'm serious! Because if you want more, quit complaining about the job you've got—there are plenty of people sleeping under a bridge who don't have one. Quit complaining about the stuff you have; thank God for it. When you wake up and your feet hit the floor, say, "Father God, I thank you for the car that I've got. I thank you for the house I'm in. I thank you for this bed I'm sleeping in. I thank you for these covers I have. I thank you for these 800-thread-count Egyptian cotton sheets that my butt is sliding out of. Lord, I thank you!"

Imagine this—I heard somebody say one time, "What if all you had today was what you thanked God for yesterday?"

God doesn't want your inferior stuff. He doesn't want sloppiness from you. He doesn't want your leftovers. *God wants your best.* And in turn, He says, "If you honor Me, I'll honor you. But if you think everything concerning Me is light, if you take everything of Mine so lightly, then I'll lightly esteem you." And he used the word *despise.* To not recognize how important God is—He called that *despising.*

There's nothing more important to me. My *wife* is not more important to me than God. My *child* is not more important to me than God.

I thank God *for* my wife; I thank God *for* my child—but they are not above God.

God always comes first.

I love all of you! But you will never come before God.

---

[8] A car, especially an old or dilapidated one.

I love the businesses God has blessed me with. They will never come before God.

Nothing inferior is going to be offered to God from my side. That's my way of honoring Him.

Everything I offer Him has to have value to it.

Here's one last thing to help you: If I value an iPad,[9] and I give it to someone—do you know they may not like Apple products? They may prefer Android.[10]

So, they may look at what I'm giving them and say, "Well, this is an iPad tablet; I don't want this!" Do they value it? *No.*

Do I? *Yes.*

Is it important to me? *Yes.*

Is it important to them? *No.*

Notice what God said: "If *you* honor it, if it's important to *you*, then it's important to Me."

That is why the woman with the two pennies gave the same amount as the people who were pouring riches into the treasury. Because it's not about the monetary amount; it's about what *you* honor.

If it's your time, if it's your treasure, if it's your talent—will you give your best to God?

Or will you give something INFERIOR?

---

[9] iPad is a trademark of Apple Inc., registered in the U.S. and other countries.

[10] Android is a trademark of Google LLC., registered in the U.S. and other countries.

CHAPTER 3

IRREVERENCE

We are learning about the Eyes/I's of Dishonor. We talked about INTRUDING—intruding in an office that's not yours, intruding in places you weren't invited to. Some people have always got a suggestion, they've always got a thought, they've always got something they need to share with you, and you didn't ask. They've got an opinion, they've got advice, they've got counsel—whatever they want to call it—and you just didn't ask them for it. So Chapter 1 is about the concept of intruding, or being in a place where you weren't invited or should not be.

Chapter 2 discussed the idea of INFERIOR, offering something less than your best to God. God is concerned; He makes a point to concern Himself with what you value; and whatever you value, God values. So bringing God things that are inferior is a problem.

In this chapter, we'll address IRREVERENCE—a lack of reverence for the things of God, and for the people of God.

1 SAMUEL 2:29–36
Wherefore kick ye at my sacrifice and at mine offering, which I have commanded in my habitation; and honourest thy sons above me, to make yourselves fat with the chiefest of all the offerings of Israel my people? Wherefore the LORD God of Israel saith, I SAID INDEED THAT THY HOUSE, AND THE HOUSE OF THY FATHER, SHOULD WALK BEFORE ME FOR EVER: BUT NOW THE

LORD SAITH, BE IT FAR FROM ME; for THEM THAT HONOR ME I WILL HONOUR, AND THEY THAT DESPISE ME SHALL BE LIGHTLY ESTEEMED. Behold, the days come that I will cut off thine arm, and the arm of thy father's house, that there shall not be an old man in thine house. And thou shalt see an enemy in my habitation, in all the wealthy which God shall give Israel: and there shall not be an old man in thine house for ever. And the man of thine, whom I shall not cut off from mine altar, shall be to consume thine eyes, and to grieve thine heart: and all the increase of thine house shall die in the flower of their age. And this shall be a sign unto thee, that shall come upon thy two sons, on Hophni and Phinehas; in one day they shall die both of them. And I will raise me up a faithful priest, **THAT SHALL DO ACCORDING TO THAT WHICH IS IN MINE HEART AND IN MY MIND:** and I will build him a sure house; and he shall walk before mine anointed for ever. And it shall come to pass, that even one that is left in thine house shall come and crouch to him for a piece of silver and a morsel of bread, and shall say, Put me, I pray thee, into one of the priests' offices, that I may eat a piece of bread.

As we've noted, this verse is interesting because God is saying, "If you honor Me, I'll honor you. And if you don't apply honor to My name, if you lightly esteem Me, then I'll lightly esteem you." It's interesting because God is letting you know very clearly that how you treat the things of God will determine your outcome with God.

We live in a world where everything is, "Whatever." Nothing is a big deal; everything has gotten to a place of extreme casualness.

If you look in Chapter 38 of the book of Exodus, God outlined the way He expected Aaron to dress to come before Him to minister to Him. He outlined it in almost thirty verses, saying, "This is what you should wear. This is what color it should be. This is how it should be woven. This is the type of material. This is what is should look like." It matters! So when I see people in their khaki shorts and their Hawaiian shirts on the pulpit, I kinda wonder, "What is *that* all about?"

I can assure you of this much: God doesn't necessarily concern Himself with what a person wears *per se.* But the moment you become casual about what happens on the pulpit?

Everything else becomes casual with it.

And the challenge is that by and large, the body of Christ starts to see a loss of power. I'm telling you, it has everything to do with a lack of honor.

When I was a kid, when we went to church, we wore church clothes! You didn't wear your church clothes in the street, you wore them to church. And when you came home, you changed out of your church clothes into your street clothes, and *then* you'd run around and get dirty!

Now listen, "Come as you are" is not a statement regarding how you dress.

"Come as you are" means come in the *spiritual condition* in which you are—and if you don't have any knowledge of what you should do or what's appropriate, come on!

Our 1 Samuel passage is saying that those who will do life the way that's in God's heart and His mind, those are the people He considers faithful—not the ones who want to do it their way and force God into it!

See, this is the place where we have to learn what our responsibilities are and how to be honorable. And I honestly believe that one of the major problems people face today is a lack of honor concerning the things of God, concerning the people of God, concerning the church of God.

There's just no honor!

And honor will change your behavior. Honor will cause you to do things differently.

So He's telling the priest Eli and his family, "You were my chosen people. Your family was the one I chose. I was gonna set up your house forever, but because of the choices you're making? I changed My mind. Now what I'm gonna do is I'm gonna raise up somebody else who's going to do things the way I ask them to do it, and your house, your family is going to crouch and beg them for bread."

Not only did it affect them, it affected their children, their inheritance, and their lineage—that's crazy!

All because of a lack of faithfulness and a lack of honor. So many people struggle with the concept of honor because they think, "Well, I didn't do anything specific to you. I just … didn't do anything!" And that's what He's talking about! When you lightly esteem Him, He calls it dishonor.

Dishonor is not the result of you having done something or said something specific that causes dishonor. Dishonor is immediately applied when there is no honor. To honor something means you make it weighty, you make it important, you make it significant. Wherever there is no honor, no value, no esteem, there is immediate dishonor.

When you make it important, God says, "I'll make *you* important. When you honor the things concerning Me, then I'll honor you."

When you give it no weight, when it's not important to you, then guess what happens?

There's a struggle.

2 TIMOTHY 3:1-9
This know also, that in the last days perilous times shall come. For men shall be of their own selves, covetous, boasters, proud, blasphemers, disobedient to parents, unthankful, unholy, without natural affection, trucebreakers, false accusers, incontinent, fierce, despisers of those that are good, traitors, heady, highminded, lovers of pleasure more than lovers of God; having a form of godliness, but denying the power thereof: from such turn away. For of this sort are they which creep into houses, and lead captive silly women laden with sins, led away with divers lusts, ever learning, and never able to come to the knowledge of the truth. Now as Jannes and Jambres withstood Moses, so do these also resist the truth: men of corrupt minds, reprobate concerning the faith. But they shall proceed no further: for their folly shall be manifest unto all men, as theirs also was."

Isn't that something? He said they wouldn't even have natural affection toward their *families*.

God gave me my family—he gave me my wife, he gave me my child. As the man, I am responsible for protecting them. So everything that I do, I no longer do for myself. I do it because I have to protect the family God has given me. And if I love my family, I don't put them in jeopardy, I don't put them in places of hurt, and I don't put them in places of trouble because I have a natural affection for them!

I really struggle when I see some of you ladies get hooked up with worthless men. If he wants to play video games all day and has nothing in him that desires to protect you as his wife, he doesn't have natural affection. There's something wrong with that!

Natural affection says, "I protect *everything* concerning my house —my children, my wife, my family—because I have a natural love for them, and I want the best for them." Do you understand what I'm trying to say?

These "last days" are going to be violent times! The things we see and hear about on the news—it's *crazy* out there! We are not blindly unaware of what's going on. The Bible says these things would come to pass. It says people will curse their parents, show no gratitude, and have no respect for what is holy!

PROVERBS 30:17
The eye that mocketh at his father, and despiseth to obey his mother, the ravens of the valley shall pick it out, and the young eagles shall eat it.

Look at this—I think sometimes we don't understand how God sees things. And sometimes when referring to the Old Testament, people go, "Well, that's *Old* Testament."

God never changes. And if He didn't like it in the Old Testament, He doesn't like it today! Just because you've been redeemed from some things, doesn't mean that He has forgotten and changed His mind about what He likes and does not like.

Our verses from 1 Timothy say that children will curse their parents, right? Watch this: *"The eye that mocketh at his father."* You know what that means?

Your kids are rolling their eyes at you!

And you let it slide because you think it's cute. "Oh, they just have *personality.* They're just coming into their own."

Look at what God says: "The eye that mocketh at his father and despises to obey his mother, THE RAVENS OF THE VALLEY SHALL PICK IT OUT, AND THE YOUNG EAGLES SHALL EAT IT."

God says this about just rolling your eyes? Yes, the ravens will pluck 'em out and the eagles will *eat* your eyes.

Y'all better get that stuff under control! The parents are the first form of authority that a child sees. And if your child has no respect for you, when they get into school and start acting a fool, they'll have no respect for authority, for the police. My grandma used to say, "I beat you so the cops don't have to. Because the difference between me and the Po-Po? It's that I know when to stop, and they don't!"

I need you to understand something; I'm not advocating abusing your kids. What I *am* advocating is teaching them honor. And for them to roll their eyes at you, which you may dismiss as something that is insignificant? That is a measure of their heart toward you.

My mother would smack the taste outta your mouth!

For real, though—she had stages!

First was a *look*. Then it was a *point*. And if she had to open her mouth, it was *on and poppin'*!

In my day, when we addressed people, it was "Sir." Even to this day, I still say "Sir."

"Yes, Sir."

"No, Sir."

Whether they are above me, beneath me, younger than me, older than me—doesn't even matter.

And I people say to me, "Sir? Who's Sir? It's *you*!

"No, Sir's my dad."

No, Sir is *you*.

"You don't have to call me that." I didn't call you that for you!

Me being honorable has nothing to do with you!

And if God sees *rolling the eyes*?

Let's go back to 2 Timothy 3:1-5. What does it say people will be like? Lovers of their own selves, covetous, boasters, proud, blasphemers, disobedient to parents, unthankful, unholy, Without natural affection, truce breakers, false accusers, incontinent, fierce, despisers of those that are good, traitors, heady, lovers of pleasures more than lovers of God; having a form of godliness, but denying the power thereof.

You know what self-control is?

Self-control says, "I will not allow my body to do things that I did not permit it to do."

That's self-control.

The Bible says one of the fruits of the spirit is to be *temperate*—it's to have that level of self-control that says, "I don't do things because my friends do it, I don't do things because the world says it's okay, I do what *I know* is right." As Paul would say, "I beat my body into subjection. My body will not tell *me* what *it's* going to do; *I'm* going to tell *it* what to do. And as I tell it what to do, it must obey."[11]

Some people have no self-control. None whatsoever.

You have to be reckless, and you have to be conceited to love pleasure more than God. So many people don't understand this. Narcissistic people will put their *whole family* in jeopardy so that *they* can do the things *they* want to do. Narcissistic people love themselves. They're so conceited that life is all about what *they* want, what *they're* willing to do, what *they* like, and everybody around them is going to have to suffer because they cannot put anybody else above them.

Notice the order in our scripture passage! God says they're selfish because they're lovers of pleasure more than God, and that makes them reckless.

---

[11] 1 Corinthians 9:27.

Nothing worse than a reckless person!

You can't be in my life and be reckless. Do you want to know why? Because Satan is always looking for an opportunity—he's just waiting for you to do something dumb. He's got a plan! Everybody thinks it's God sitting there with a mallet, waiting to bust you upside the head. It's not God; it's Satan waitin'!

He's like, "Just do something dumb. All you've gotta do is do it and I'm gonna jump all in there!" That's why the Bible says, "Give him no place."[12]

So many people want to blame demons, or the devil—"Pastor, the devil made me do it."

The Bible says the spirit of the prophet is subject to the prophet.[13] If you go around saying, "Oh, the Holy Ghost guided me and just took over," you're lying. You just called the Holy Ghost witchcraft. You just called something holy profane, because the spirit of the prophet is subject to the prophet.

Years ago, there was someone in our church who'd start screaming every time I would get to preaching. And I confronted them about it. I said, "You're causing a distraction. All we can hear when we listen to the audio recording is you."

"Well, I just, y'know, I get the Spirit!"

No, the Spirit is subject to *you*.

Don't tell me that the Holy Ghost is causing this disruption; it's *you*, and *your* flesh.

People don't understand that a lot of times, the problem is not *anything related* to demonic influence. It's you loving yourself so

---

12 Ephesians 4:27.

13 1 Corinthians 14:32.

much that you put everything at risk. When you love yourself so much, you love pleasure more than you love God. Because if you love God, if you *truly* love God, you will have better self-control.

According to 2 Timothy 3, these people will *appear* to have a godly life, but they will not let the power of God change them. They *appear* to have a godly life, but they spend so much time keeping up appearances, yet they're not really changed. If you want to know who a person really is, let 'em hit bottom. Everybody can "fake the funk on a nasty dunk" when they are doing all right! But the moment all hell breaks loose, that's when you'll see who you're really dealing with. That's when you'll see what a person is really all about. If it's alcohol, that'll become the thing. When they hit bottom, they'll go to that, not God!

When all hell breaks loose in *my* life? There's only one place I know to go. I've been to all the other places! I don't know about you, but some people say: "I'm so glad I'm not what I used to be. And I might not be where I need to be, but I'm so glad I don't look like what I've been through!" It's really that simple for me!

So as we begin to understand honor, we live differently. We don't live a life of *IRREVERENCE* toward the things of God, toward the people of God.

Notice how the proverb said just *mocking* your parents, rolling your eyes, is a problem. That's a level of honor toward the people in your life!

ROMANS 13:7
Render therefore to all their dues: tribute to whom tribute is due; custom to whom custom; fear to whom fear; honor to whom honour.

One translation of this verse says something like, "If you have a bill, pay it," That's what it means!

See, so many people don't understand this idea because they're so disrespectful toward debts they owe. Not only just honor, not only just respect—a lot of people *regard* God, but they don't *respect* God.

So He says, "Pay *all* that is owed to them." It could be taxes—pay all that's owed. If it be revenue—money—if you owe a bill, pay it. The GOD'S WORD translation says, "If you owe tolls, pay them. If you owe someone respect, respect that person. If you owe someone honor, honor that person."

People have to recognize what "honorable" looks like. Because when you're honorable concerning the things in your life, then you're honorable concerning your bills, you're honorable concerning your debts, you're honorable concerning what you owe—not just from a money standpoint, but even from an honor standpoint!

Wives, do you honor your husband? Because the Bible says he's owed honor. Not because he's the greatest husband in the world, not because he was especially good today—but you'll be intimate with him today because as your husband, he deserves the honor.

And husbands—you know I wasn't going to let you off the hook! The Bible says you are to love your wife. You are to love her the same way Christ loves the church—Christ didn't cheat on the church!

When you honor something, you give it value. You esteem it, you give it weight, it's important to you. When you find something you honor, it's so important to you that *you* decrease as you magnify *it*.

And as you decrease, you become less concerned with keeping count and keeping score, and you become more concerned with "how do I value this, how do I make this weighty, how do I deal with this?"

Way too many people are disrespectful from the standpoint of honor toward their pastors and leaders! I have experienced many times when people are *so dishonorable* and don't even know it. I don't normally point it out; I just let it slide because it affects them more than it affects me.

2 KINGS 1:6–15
And they said unto him, There came a man up to meet us, and said unto us, Go, turn again unto the king that send you, and say unto him, Thus saith the LORD, Is it not because there is not a God in Israel, that thou sendest to enquire of Baalzebub the god of Ekron? Therefore thou shalt not come down from that bed on which thou art gone up, but shalt surely die. And he said unto them, What manner of man was he which came up to meet you, and told you these words? And they answered him, He was an hairy man, and girt with a girdle of leather about his loins. And he said, It is Elijah the Tishbite. Then the king sent unto him a captain of fifty with his fifty. And he went up to him: and, behold, he sat on the top of an hill. And he spake unto him, Thou man of God, the king hath said, Come down. And Elijah answered and said to the captain of the fifty, If I be a man of God, then let fire come down from heaven, and consume thee and thy fifty. And there came down fire from heaven, and consumed him and his fifty. Again also he sent unto him another captain of fifty with his fifty. And he answered and said unto him, O man of God, thus hath the king said, Come down quickly. And Elijah answered and said unto them, If I be a man of God, let fire come down from heaven, and consume thee and thy fifty. And the fire of God came down from heaven, and consumed him and his fifty. And he sent again a captain of the third fifty with his fifty. And the third captain of fifty went up, and came and fell on his knees before Elijah, and besought him, and said unto him, O man of God, I pray thee, let my life, and the life of these fifty thy servants, be precious in thy sight. And the angel of the LORD said unto Elijah, Go down with him: be not afraid of him. And he arose, and went down with him unto the king.

Those first two clowns in this passage had no idea how to approach a man of God! They came talking about "The king told me to tell you. …" I don't care what the king told you to tell me!

If I be what you said I am? *Poof.* Cash me outside.[14]

It's funny how the third captain came and bowed his knee, like "Elijah, please—listen, bruh. We already heard what happened to the other two, so I ain't trying to tell you to do anything, I'm coming to *ask*."

We laugh, but there's a principle here—it's honor. It's how you approach people.

If someone is, in fact, a woman of God or a man of God; how do you approach them?

"Well, they're just like me!" No, really, they're not.

I've had so many people call me just Gene. They won't even call me Pastor Gene. Not my problem! I know my supply. That's why Paul said, "*I magnify my office.*"[15] Paul didn't magnify himself! Remember he said, "I count it as dung (and if you don't know what dung is, it's doo-doo!) but I do magnify my office. I am called as an apostle, I understand my authority in what God has called me to do, and what God is doing inside me."

So many people don't understand how to deal with the things of God, how to deal with the people of God. It's important, it matters! If it matters to God, it should matter to you.

MARK 6:2
And when the sabbath day was come, he began to teach in the synagogue: and many hearing him were

---

[14] Originating as the catchphrase of TV and social-media star Danielle Bregoli, *cash me outside* is a phrase challenging another person, often humorously, to a fight. (https://www.dictionary.com/e/memes/cash-me-outside/)

[15] Romans 11:13.

astonished, saying, From whence hath this man these things? And what wisdom is this which is given unto him, that even such mighty works are wrought by his hands? Is not this the carpenter, the son of Mary, the brother of James, and Joses, and of Judas, and Simon? And are not his sisters here with us? And they were offended at him. But Jesus said unto them, A prophet is not without honour, but in his own country, and among his own kin, and in his own house. And HE COULD THERE DO NO MIGHTY WORK, save that he laid his hands upon a few sick folk, and healed them. And he marveled because of their unbelief. And he went round about the villages, teaching."

Does it say he would do no mighty works there because he was *mad*, he was salty with the people?

Does it say that He said, "You know what? You wanna call me a carpenter? *Then die!*"

No, it said he *couldn't* do mighty works. The power of God was *stifled* because of how people saw Him. I want you to understand: everything Jesus did, He did as a man anointed by God. Therefore He did not do things as God in the flesh, per se. He did His works as a *man* who was anointed *by* God, who happened to reside in the flesh. So they *shut down* the King of Glory, because they wanted to rule him out as a carpenter! This is talking about His brothers, His sisters— *what does that have to do with anything?*

I've had people ask me "How old are you?" That's none of your business! Either I'm anointed, or I'm not. Stop trying to know men after the flesh. I'm serious, people do that! How old I am is none of your business. Is that how you're trying to determine whether or not you're going to listen to what I have to say? I mean, what does that matter? I have gray hairs! And if we can be honest, one of them is because of you!

You know when Jesus says that *"a prophet is not WITHOUT HONOR"*? That phrase, "without honor," means to *despise*, to make little of, or to ignore.

Let's go back to that: *"But Jesus said unto them, A prophet is not without honour, but in his own country, and among his own kin, and in his own house" (Mark 6:4).*

In other words, *only people in his own house* will make little of a prophet. Only people of his *own kin* will despise a prophet. Only people of his own house, his own family, will ignore the fact that he's a prophet!

Here Jesus has been sent to bring healing and deliverance, to set them free—and they can't even recognize the man.

Mark 6:2 says:

> **And when the sabbath day was come, he began to teach in the synagogue: and many hearing him were astonished, saying, From whence hath this man these things? And what wisdom is this which is given unto him, that even such mighty works are wrought by his hands?**

They were wondering where Jesus was getting these things He was teaching about. Where did that wisdom come from? Where did the power come from? They didn't have a problem recognizing *God;* they had a problem recognizing God in the *Man,* and it tripped them up! It tripped them up something serious.

> **1 THESSALONIANS 5:12**
> **And we beseech you, brethren, TO KNOW THEM WHICH LABOUR AMONG YOU, AND ARE OVER YOU IN THE LORD, AND ADMONISH YOU; AND TO ESTEEM THEM VERY HIGHLY IN LOVE FOR THEIR WORK'S SAKE. And be at peace among yourselves.**

So those who labor among you, if they are over you in the Lord, they are to *admonish* you.

Do you know what "admonishment" means? It means *correction.*[16] It means smacking you upside your little peanut head when you need it, so you can get right and get it together!

He said you are to *know them.* Do you know what "to know them" means? It means to recognize who they are, and to value or to esteem their whole purpose—which is to admonish you—and to esteem them very highly in love.

Why?

For the work!

For what reason?

For the sake of the work.

What work?

Admonishing you!

"To esteem them." Do you know what "esteem" means? It means *I value you more than me.*

"Esteem them"—why?

For the work that they do.

Nothing irritates me more than seeing a minister criticize another minister for what they're doing. A minister should know how hard it is to do the work of ministry! *They should know.*

Y'all have no idea the attack I've had to endure recently— physically, emotionally, health-wise—because the more light a minister brings, the more of a target he or she becomes.

---

16 "Admonish," *Merriam-Webster*, Merriam-Webster, www.merriam-webster.com/ dictionary/admonish.

That's why Paul said, "I besought the Lord three times, but there was a messenger of Satan sent to buffet me."[17] And he explained the reason for the attack from Satan: it was for the abundance of revelation.

See, this is where the strong and the weak are separated. Because the truth of the matter is just because you see the revelation on Wednesday night and Sunday morning does not mean that's where it began and where it ended.

Paul said you are to esteem God's laborers because of the *work they do*—the stuff you *don't* see—the middle-of-the-night phone calls, the problems that get laid on them to help other people resolve—*for the work's sake.* You don't know the totality of the work! You don't know the times where we've had to do things for other people that we can't even do for ourselves!

People deserve some honor just because of the work they do, the profession they have chosen, the occupation they have submitted themselves to! That's why God's Word said to esteem them in love and be at peace among yourselves.

You want to know why some people don't have any peace? *Because they won't esteem those that are over them in the Lord.* They don't value the laborers for the work's sake. Listen to me: if your shepherd, your pastor, is the bishop of your soul? Then that person has a responsibility to protect you and to wage war on your behalf, even when you don't know it. So many people find themselves in predicaments they could have avoided if they had learned to respect not only their pastor, but also their church.

If you don't believe me, then riddle me this: When Paul said of the man who slept with his father's wife, "Put him out of the church, turn him over to Satan for the destruction of his flesh, for the saving of his

---

[17] 2 Corinthians 12:8.

soul,"[18]—Why would they have to put him outside the fellowship? Because within the church, there is protection. And Paul said, "You've got to put him *outside* so Satan can do whatever he wants to do." I guarantee you, when Satan attacks someone's life, the first stage that person goes through is forgetting *who* and *what* their supply really is. They place no value on their church; they place no value on their responsibility to serve in their church, to give to their church, to attend their church. And then they wonder why they are outside getting their brains beat in, because they have no regard, no honor!

HEBREWS 13:17
Obey them that have the rule over you, and submit yourselves: for they watch for your souls, as they that must give account, that they may do it with joy, and not with grief: for that is unprofitable for you.

Who has to give an account? Your pastor(s)?

You mean to tell me that we pastors have to give an account? For *you, the people in our church*? We have to watch for your soul, and give an account for you?

Awwww, man, come on! As they say in the West Indies, "Stop tell lie and pick up teeth!"

Notice that it says I should do that with joy! And not with grief, because that is unprofitable for *you*. Not me!

You know, I made it a point never to be a burden to my pastor. There were times when I needed help, and there were times when I asked for help, and I needed counseling, and I needed different things, spiritual guidance and all that. Don't get me wrong, I had those moments! But you know, when those moments came, I always made it so that *I* was a blessing to *him*.

---

[18] 1 Corinthians 5:5

For instance, I took him out to his favorite restaurant, and *then* I said "Hey, can I ask you a question? While you're enjoying this steak, this filet mignon, because I want to be a blessing to you and I want this to be with joy—" Y'all need to understand. I'm trying to teach you something! Because when people come with honor, pastors don't mind helping people who are honorable. What strikes a sour note is people giving them grief!

I always made it a priority not to be a burden. I watched other people be burdens, and I said, "I'm going to make it so that *he* calls *me* because I'm easy to talk to. I'm going to make it so that he *wants* to be around me because I'm always a blessing."

Listen, people are people. They're human. Everybody wants to know they're appreciated. Everybody wants to know they're valued. You catch way more flies with honey than you do with vinegar!

1 TIMOTHY 5:17
Let the elders that rule well be counted worthy of double honour, especially they who labour in the word and doctrine.

You know what I love about my church? We don't have much problem with this. But I know churches—I really do—whose pastor has to live off of more faith than the people are willing to live off of.

Can you imagine going to work where people were sitting around talking about your salary? Think about it! You go to work tomorrow; you walk in the door, and people are having a meeting about *your* salary. Some think you make too much; some think you make too little; some think you have too much stuff; some think maybe they should go to you and get something from you because hey, you make a good salary. You'd be like, "Hold up!"

And then Pastor Appreciation Month comes around, and people struggle with donating to that—and it's only one time a year! And they're like, "Oh, well, I give my tithe." Your tithe doesn't go to your pastor; your tithe goes to running the church.

How do you define "adequate"?

Let's say it takes $5,000 to run your pastor's house on a monthly basis. I don't know what it costs; I'm just throwing out a number here, but let's say it takes $5,000 to run his home. How much is adequate?

Let's say it takes $10,000 to run *one* home. How much is adequate?

If it takes $5,000 to run another home, what is adequate? *$5,000.*

If it takes $10,000 to run the first home, what is adequate? *$10,000.*

So then "adequate" is not a specific *number;* "adequate" is based on what a person *needs.*

The Bible says, "Desire the best gift."[19] What is the best gift? *The one you need at the time.*

If you're going to fight the good fight, what is the good fight? *The one you win.*

What defines adequate for *me* is not adequate for everyone, nor is it subject to your determination of what is adequate! What's adequate is *what it takes.*

Our passage says, "Let them be worthy of *double* honor." So *now* if it takes $5,000 to run your house, what is *double* honor? *$10,000.*

Paul cracks me up in this verse. He's like, "So I'm-a tell you this, but then I'm-a give you some scripture so y'all can't act like I'm making this up!"

---

[19] 1 Corinthians 10:31.

When you buy food at a restaurant, do you know you're paying for spoilage? Not that the food you *get* is spoiled, but spoilage is considered in that price. Let's say the restaurant buys fifty chickens; not all fifty of those chickens are going to be served. At some point, they might look at a chicken and say, "We're not serving this one. And that chicken over there has been here too long, so we're not serving that one" … you hope!

I'm letting you in on a little secret: You know those rotisserie chickens that are already cooked? I'm not going to tell you they're *bad*, but I *am* going to tell you they're the ones that have been sitting there for a minute! That was a brilliant idea. That's how we get rid of spoilage! And then you go and buy it, take it home, and feed it to your kids instead of taking a chicken, rubbing it down with some salt, putting a little olive oil on it, stuffing it with some herbs, throwing it in the oven, and 45 minutes later, you have a fresh roasted chicken. Never mind, here's what I'm trying to tell you! They factor in *loss* into their prices, because there's *always* going to be some loss. Right?

So when Paul talks about the ox treading out the corn,[20] he's saying a working animal has to eat in order to live. But they *know* an animal cannot eat *all* of what it's given—only what it needs to sustain its energy to keep plowing—in order to keep giving the farmer what he needs. So if you *muzzle* the ox, then the ox doesn't have enough energy to continue plowing because you are starving the ox! In other words, if you make the pastor worry about *his* finances instead of being wholly focused on preaching and teaching, Pastor has to figure out how to get *his* bills paid, how to meet *his* needs. And church people say, "Just trust God!"

---

[20] 1 Corinthians 9:9.

See how that works? You have to understand, it's not easy! An attack comes with this attitude toward the pastor's finances; a fight comes with it.

So Paul tells the Corinthians, "That's why the scripture says, 'Don't muzzle the ox when it's treading out the corn.'" He even says that those who preach the gospel should live off of the gospel.[21] It's sad that some pastors have to have businesses and other jobs in order to provide for their family because their church struggles with giving.

Isn't that something?

You never know how much junk you have until you have to move it! When we first moved into our current home, my wife and I thought about hiring a lady who was a professional organizer to organize our kitchen. She was referred by another minister friend of mine. So I called her up and I said, "Hey, what do you charge to do your work?"

She said, "Well, I primarily work with ministers, and I kinda just let them decide because I know ministers don't have money."

I was like, *Skrrrt!* Pump your brakes, lady!

I said, "What do you charge non-ministers?"

She said, "I don't want to tell you that."

I said, "Then we won't be working together."

When she asked me why, I said, "Because the laborer is worthy of his hire, and if you can't tell me what you charge, we won't be doing business together!"

It *literally* took a fight to get her to even say what she normally charges, so we ended up not doing it. See, in her mind, no minister has

---

21 1 Corinthians 9:14.

money. And in my mind, the devil is a liar! I have a supply, and my supply doesn't have to hurt *you* in order for it to work.

That's why the Bible says, "Render therefore to all their dues: tribute to whom tribute is due; custom to whom custom; fear to whom fear; honour to whom honour."[22] Whatever is owed, do it! Because it takes the same amount of faith for me to believe God for the total amount than it does for me to beat you up, hurt you, take from you.

You mean to tell me that the CEO of Coca-Cola, who makes millions of dollars a year selling sugar water should be better paid than —let's not even talk about pastors, let's talk about our teachers! Our teachers get paid *peanuts* to deal with your bad children. Yet kids idolize basketball stars, who do absolutely nothing to contribute to the overall well-being of society! They love, and honor, and chase after, and want to emulate *them*, and yet they have *no* regard for their teachers.

You guys have got to understand there's a problem with the way people see things! And we have to be the ones who teach them better, to say, "This is not the way this is going to be."

---

[22] Romans 13:7.

THE EYES OF HONOR: THE CURRENCY OF HEAVEN

CHAPTER 4

INDICTMENT

Let's go back to 1 Samuel 2:29–36:

> Wherefore kick ye at my sacrifice and at mine offering, which I have commanded in my habitation; and honourest thy sons above me, to make yourselves fat with the chiefest of all the offerings of Israel my people? Wherefore the LORD God of Israel saith, I said indeed that thy house, and the house of thy father, should walk before me for ever: but now the LORD saith, Be it far from me; for them that honour me I will honour, and they that despise me shall be lightly esteemed. Behold, the days come that I will cut off thine arm, and the arm of thy father's house, that there shall not be an old man in thine house. And thou shalt see an enemy in my habitation, in all the wealthy which God shall give Israel: and there shall not be an old man in thine house for ever. And the man of thine, whom I shall not cut off from mine altar, shall be to consume thine eyes, and to grieve thine heart: and all the increase of thine house shall die in the flower of their age. And this shall be a sign unto thee, that shall come upon thy two sons, on Hophni and Phinehas; in one day they shall die both of them. And I will raise me up a faithful priest, that shall do according to that which is in mine heart and in my mind: and I will build him a sure house; and he shall walk before mine anointed for ever. And it shall come to pass,

that every one that is left in thine house shall come and crouch to him for a piece of silver and a morsel of bread, and shall say, Put me, I pray thee, into one of the priests' offices, that I may eat a piece of bread.

We see some very clear things here in this passage. Firstly, we see that God had a plan for Eli's family, and because of how they handled things, that plan changed. God said, "My intention was to take care of your house forever, but because of how you acted and how you handled things, now be it far from Me. This is not gonna happen!"

And notice the reason He gave: "You valued your kids more than you valued Me. You honored your children more than you honor the things I brought to your life."

He said, "If you honor Me, then I'll honor you. But if you lightly esteem Me, then I'll lightly esteem you."

I've said this before, and I mean it: Honor is a lost art today. People are just not honorable like they used to be. It's funny because Dad Hagin prophesied that things would change, and we wouldn't see as many miracles as we used to because of the fact that honor has been lost.

If you don't honor the things of God, you'll find something more important to do than serve. If you don't honor the things of God, you'll find something more important to do than to show up at a Wednesday night service.

When you honor the things of God, you put the things of God *first*; and making them your priority displays your honor toward the things that God has for you. That's why He said, "I'll raise me up a *faithful* priest." If you recall, the definition of "faithful" is "doing something the way it is in *God's* heart, and in *God's* mind." *That* makes you faithful. You can quote scripture until you're blue in the face—doesn't make you faithful! You can exercise what you believe to be faith, and be *full* of faith, and still not be faithful!

There is a way God's things are supposed to be handled. I've watched so many people struggle with trying to figure out, "How do I get this to work, how do I make this happen, how do I do such and such? I've got millions and millions of questions, Pastor, why is this not happening?" *Because you're not doing it the way God wants it done.*

It's very simple! Because either *you're* wrong, or *God's* wrong.

Now, I'm not a betting kind of man—but my money's on God!

So you can do whatever *you* think, but it doesn't make it *godly.*

So many people think, "If I can just do what *I* want to do, somehow God will put His stamp on it."

If you notice in our passage, their dishonor not only cost *them,* but their *children.* It cost his *and* his children's lives, it cost them the prosperity *of their whole House.* Their *generations* were affected because of *their* lack of honor. You have to understand, and you've got to get this because it is so significant for our ability to walk in God's favor and God's honor. See, when you are not struggling like everybody else is, that's God honoring you! When you seem to come into situations in which God blesses you, and other people don't get that blessing? That's God honoring *you!* And if you want to be honored *by* God, you'd better be honorable toward Him!

Honor means to apply weight to something. Picture the Scales of Justice—whatever is weightier (or heavier) tips the scales to its side. *That is honor.* That's what honor means! It means you give *so much* weight to it that nothing else weighs more than it. You make it so weighty in your life that there's nothing else more important. When you honor God, then you put the things of God first and foremost.

Some people try to get closer to *me,* they want to talk to *me,* they want to hang out with *me,* but they don't serve. We have nothing in common! I value the things of God. If you want to hang out with *me*, show up on a work day!

"Well, Pastor, I just wanted to hang out and talk to you, I've got millions of questions." So what? You'll still have them!

Some of you singles would do well to recognize that, too. If you've got someone who is interested in you, but they won't show up to volunteer on a church work day like you do? They ain't interested! Or at least they're not interested in the things *you're* interested in.

Many people want access, but they don't want to pay the *price* for access—it's a lack of honor toward the things of God. You don't get in just 'cause you think you're cute, and you don't get in because you think you're anointed! You get in because there's a cost to be paid. So honor comes into that place where we begin to realize what's important and what's valuable. If we have anything in common, then what *I* honor, *you'll* honor. What *I* value, *you'll* value.

2 TIMOTHY 3:1–9 (GW)
You must understand this: In the last days there will be violent periods of time. People will be selfish and love money. They will brag, be arrogant, and use abusive language. They will curse their parents, show no gratitude, have no respect for what is holy, and lack normal affection for their families. They will refuse to make peace with anyone. THEY WILL BE SLANDEROUS, LACK SELF-CONTROL, BE BRUTAL, AND HAVE NO LOVE FOR WHAT IS GOOD. They will be traitors. They will be reckless and conceited. They will love pleasure rather than God. They will appear to have a godly life, but they will not let its power change them. Stay away from such people. Some of these men go into homes and mislead weak-minded women who are burdened with sins and led by all kinds of desires. These women are always studying but are never able to recognize the truth. As Jannes and Jambres opposed Moses, so these men oppose

the truth. Their minds are corrupt, and the faith they teach is counterfeit. Certainly, they won't get very far. Like the stupidity of Jannes and Jambres, their stupidity will be plain to everyone.

We examined this passage earlier. But now we're emphasizing *"They will refuse to make peace with anyone. They will be slanderous, lack self-control, brutal, and have no love for what is good."* The "I" of this chapter is INDICTMENT, which means "to bring charges against," because one of the things that is absolutely rooted in dishonor is how you deal with other people in the body.

MATTHEW 7:1
Judge not, that ye be not judged. For with what judgement ye judge, ye shall be judged: and with what measure ye mete, it shall be measured to you again.

Notice Jesus said, in other words, "The measure you use to judge others is the same measure that is used to judge *you*." Now, a *measure* is very simple. If I come to you with a teaspoon and I say, "Can I borrow a cup of sugar," we're gonna be going back and forth for a minute! Why?

Because the measure I'm asking for is not the measure I've brought.

People can be so critical of everything. They've got an opinion about everything; they've got something to say to you about everything. It is remarkable how many people deal with me when something goes wrong—but they don't usually deal with me when something goes right!

People don't come up to me and say, "You know what, Pastor? You *slammed* that message today, that was *great!*"

No, I usually get something like, "You know, Pastor, I don't understand this; I don't agree with that; I don't like such and such; this happened; something's wrong; I'm just bringing it to your attention." No, you're really being judgmental.

"Well y'know, Pastor, So-and-so did such-and-such, and ...."

You know how kids will say, "Don't judge me"? Kids will say that, right?

Okay, now listen to me—if they're *your kids?* You have authority and dominion and the right to judge *anything* concerning that which is in your sphere of responsibility. So when kids say stupid stuff like that, you pop 'em upside the head! Like, *"Who are you talking to? I'm your* judge, jury, *and* executioner! I brought you into this world; I'll take you out of it and make another one that looks just like you!"

If it's your company, you have the right to judge all that happens in your company. If it's your house, you have every right to judge what's in your house. But you *don't* have a right to what's judge *outside* your sphere of responsibility.

So the Bible says, "Wives, be subject to your *own* husbands."

"Well, I don't like the way the First Lady dresses." *Ha!*

It's funny how people can be so critical, and have opinions about lots of things that have nothing to do with them. They rail INDICTMENT and don't even know it. They're being dishonorable; there's no honor in it.

Honor would say, "Look, if it doesn't concern me, then the measure with which I'm going to judge what doesn't concern me is going to be as small as possible so that when people judge *me*, it can be as small as possible, too." Jesus said the same measure that *you dole out,* is the same measuring stick that God then takes and says, "Oh, okay, so this is the one I'm going to use when I deal with you."

This is why He's so clear about dealing with what's in your own eye first. He didn't say you couldn't help your brother deal with his problem; He said, "Deal with yours first, *then* you go."

So many people have something to say about everything. There used to be a person here—who is not here anymore—who had a problem with how another person dressed.

And I was like, *what business is it of yours?* Are you going to take them to a store and buy them something? Because if you're not, if you're not bringing solutions—look, any idiot can bring you a problem. I can't *stand* people who just report problems. I don't need a reporter! Nobody sends for a problem, they send for a *solution*.

But so many people have this thing in them that makes them want to say, "Well, the way *I* think it should be done is …."

Nobody cares. It doesn't matter!

ROMANS 14:1–10
Him that is weak in the faith receive ye, but not to doubtful disputations. For one believeth that he may eat all things: another, who is weak, eateth herbs. Let not him that eateth despise him that eateth not; and let not him which eateth not judge him that eateth: for God hath received him. Who art thou that judgest another man's servant? to his own master he standeth or falleth. Yea, he shall be holden up: for God is able to make him stand. One man esteemeth one day above another: another esteemeth every day alike. Let every man be fully persuaded in his own mind. He that regardeth the day, regardeth it unto the Lord; and he that regardeth not the day, to the Lord he doth not regard it. He that eateth, eateth to the Lord, for he giveth God thanks; and he that eateth not, to the Lord he eateth not, and giveth God thanks. For none of us liveth to himself, and no man dieth to himself. For whether we live, we live unto the Lord; and whether we die, we die unto the Lord: whether we live therefore, or die, we are the Lord's For to this end Christ both died, and rose, and revived, that he might be Lord both of the dead and living. But why dost thou judge thy brother? or

why dost thou set at nought thy brother? for we shall all stand before the judgment seat of Christ.

Notice whom He's talking to here, because He's calling them "Brethren." He's talking to the church; He's talking to believers! So what is He saying? There's one who observes a day of feasting, or a day of a particular religious calendar, or whatever they may observe that they may call holy, and another one doesn't. He said one may eat a certain way, and the other one may not.

He said *it is not your place* to judge another man's servant, because the difference between you and the one who judges is the strength or the maturity of your faith.

I don't have opinions about what other people do in their pulpits. For example, if you want to wear a Hawaiian shirt and khaki shorts in your pulpit, do what you want. I'm not doing that. God has talked to *me* about honor. God has dealt with me *personally* about honor. I am not going to tell *you* what *you* have to do. What I *can* tell you is you won't be on *this* pulpit, the one that *I* have responsibility for, unless you are honorable in your dress. But I have nothing to say to you about your pulpit.

People will post on Facebook stuff like, "Look at this church, look at this leader, look at this person, look what they're doing, look what So-and-so's doing!" *Who are you to judge another man's servant?*

And if you *do* have a revelation that is higher than someone else's revelation, then you walk in *your* revelation and allow the other person to come up in theirs.

Maybe God is working on them, because to *Him* they will stand or fall—*God* is able to hold them up.

Maybe He's taking them to the place where you are; they're just not there *yet*.

Maybe there are some things *you* need to get into *your* thick skull that He's trying to take *you* to, that *you* have not gotten yet.

But it would be better to *keep your mouth shut*, keep your mouth off of people, than it is for you to keep talking about stuff that you have no knowledge of and no authority in! That's what *gossip* is— conversing about stuff that you have no authority or right to deal with!

"Well, y'know, So-and-so did this, and *this* person does that!" Not my job.

Come on, y'all, I'm not the Holy Ghost police.

Consider this: One challenge people struggle with is what they refer to as "secular people" who do secular things; and then they'll say, "Well, isn't there a separation between what's holy and what's secular?" You know what, *if they're saved!*

I don't know where they are on their journey. The difference, I can tell you, is this: When they're public figures, their life is more public than mine is. You didn't get to see *me* when *I* did the stupid stuff they do. You didn't know me back then, when I thought like they think, when I thought the world and God *could* mix. But *who am I?* At what point in time did God appoint *me* to be the judge, jury, and executioner of all things great and small?

Notice what He said! He said those that are weak in faith, *receive them in anyway*, because to their *own* master they will rise and fall. God may be holding them up even though they're doing dumb stuff, even though they're making mistakes. God might be holding them up for a purpose and a time such as this! You have no idea what future God has planned for certain people!

I've had people call or meet with me and say, "Pastor, I messed up; I'm gonna go ahead and step down and walk away" *No, you're not!*

We're not giving up God's plan because you made a mistake! A righteous man falls *seven times*, but he gets back up, and the mature will help him get up, the mature will turn around and bring him up and take him to where he's got to go. That's what maturity is all about! Such as are mature *restore* one another, bring them back to the fullness of what God is trying to do in their life. *It is not my job to judge; it is my job to be godly!*

Some people are so brutal—they build entire platforms off of the negative. Listen, if you don't even have the basics right? *Shut up.* It's very simple!

If you can't tithe? You have nothing to say about anybody else.

If you can't even show up for church? You have *nothing* to say about anybody!

You do you. You work on *you.*

Those who are weak in faith, receive them in anyway.

Where I am is based on my *maturity*, which is why He said, "Don't judge that."

At the very end, He says, we will all stand before the judgment seat of Christ. *At the end* is when God will call you up and say, "Okay, now let's look at your *whole* life." You keep wanting to judge things in the middle! Nobody gives an award in the *middle* of the race!

You're looking at me when I might be two points down. Or when I might not have gotten my stride straight. Or when I haven't quite figured it all out yet.

But God said, "When I get done, when the *whole thing* is over, when it's all said and done and you come to the end of the line, *I'll* be the one to judge who you really are. And you might have been through some stuff, but now you have gotten it figured out. You might be 70, you might be 80, you might be 105. But at least you got it!" And by *God*, it is not your place to judge anyone in the middle!

Mind your business! Focus on *you.* Get *your* act together.

Dad Hagin was holding a convention at the Tulsa Convention Center; *thousands* of people were there. Another minister, a *very, very prominent* minister, had fallen in a very *public* way. (Anyone over 20 would know his name. It was *national* news.) It was no secret that this particular minister criticized Dad Hagin *constantly*. He called him a heretic, said things like "Faith is not real," and the "'Word of Faith' movement is false." I mean this minister just *leveled* him at all times. He happened to show up after his huge fall, and he was at a meeting there at the convention center.

The Spirit of God started to move, and this minister was just *crying* (as he was known to do!) very publicly. Dad Hagin called him up; "Come on up here, brother." Now, this guy had spoken harshly about him, tried to damage his ministry! Dad Hagin called him up and said, "This is our fellow brother in Christ. And he has made mistakes, but we need to help him restore."

He raised an offering for this man, to the tune of a couple hundred *thousand* dollars—and he gave it to him. You want to talk about a *love walk*, because I wouldn't have given him a red nickel!

Dad Hagin raised a couple hundred grand and gave it to him.

After this minister got his ministry back on track, you know, he went back to talking bad about Dad Hagin again.

Here's what I'm trying to tell you: All joking aside, I would have done the same thing. Because here's what we have to learn: living this life is a solo sport. While we work together as a team, when you stand before God, it will be only you. And He's going to wonder about *you*, He's going to ask *you;* when you stand before the judgment seat of Christ, *you* will have to give an account.

And can you *imagine* the street cred of Dad Hagin saying, "Oh yeah, I know he was talking bad about me, but I raised him 200 grand." *Do you understand the level of honor?*

This is what people don't understand: When *they've* made mistakes? They are *so clear* about grace and mercy. But when it's *somebody else?* Crucify them.

The people who shouted "Hosanna, Hosanna! Glory to the King of Kings" were the *same people* who shouted, "Crucify Him!"

You've got to know how to be honorable. You've got to keep indictment off of you.

Notice what He said to the one who honors a certain day and to the one who doesn't, to the one who eats certain foods and to the one who doesn't—He said *they're the same person.*

He said they have to be convinced in *their* minds.

So if you know to do something and *don't* do it? Now *that's* the problem.

But if you are holding to it—now, listen to me, He's not talking about doctrine. He's not talking about Bible doctrine, because I can tell you this much: Most of what people dispute over isn't Bible doctrine anyway. When have you ever seen in the Bible a church service where two songs are played, and then announcements are given, and then two more songs are played? *Never confuse liturgy with doctrine.*

Some churches will not preach on certain subjects—they'll have to answer for that.

My spiritual father told me something a long time ago. He said, "Don't be one of the ones that run around telling everybody what they're doing wrong; teach what's right. Sometimes you'll have to put a foot in the problem and a foot in the solution to get people to see it, but ultimately, what you're telling them is how to do it the right way."

A lot of people just sit back and criticize what everybody's doing.

"Oh, did you see how So-and-so did that? Did you see how this was done, did you see how that was done?" If you notice, I'm pretty silent when it comes to politics and world news. I don't have an opinion on it. Why? *Because it doesn't matter.*

It's amazing what can happen when you get focused. One thing my wife and I decided to do is minimize the hours of television we watch to an hour a day. I've read three books in two months!

You'd be shocked at how much time you have when you realize that the stuff you focus on is just not worth it.

1 CORINTHIANS 1:24–27
But unto them which are called, both Jews and Greeks, Christ the power of God, and the wisdom of God. Because the foolishness of God is wiser than men; and the weakness of God is stronger than men. For ye see your calling, brethren, how that not many wise men after the flesh, not many mighty, not many noble, are called: But God hath chosen the foolish things of the world to confound the wise; and God hath chosen the weak things of the world to confound the things which are mighty.

Notice that He says your problem is you view it after the flesh. You *just don't know* what God is doing. Who would have thought that God would use *Rahab, the whore?*

"Well, God, I don't think she's very spiritual!" He didn't care whether she was spiritual; she was *faithful.*

PROVERBS 18:13
He that answereth a matter before he heareth it, it is folly and shame unto him.

This is one of my favorite scriptures of all time.

You never answer the matter before you hear it. Don't be so quick to respond because you heard something, because you saw something. God uses the foolish things to confound the wise; you don't know the whole story! Only a *fool* answers the matter before they hear it. You have to wait sometimes!

There are a lot of things I don't understand. I'm like, "God, what in the world was *that*?"

But you know, I'm smart enough to keep my mouth shut and wait, because only a fool will open their mouth. It's better to be thought dumb and remain silent than to open your mouth and remove all doubt.

So many people are quick to give an opinion, quick to say something, quick to speak on stuff that they have *no knowledge* of.

"Well, I'm just trying to help you out." No, you're not! You're trying to find holes so that you can look like a hero, so you can find a way to be important. That's all you're doing! You're not bringing help; you're not saying, "I'll *help you* fix this; here are some solutions; I did some research to help you; look what I found! This, this, this, and this! Just want to be a blessing!"

Only a fool answers a matter before they hear it.

Sometimes a wife will come to me and talk crazy about her husband. You know, I don't care *what* she says; I don't want to answer her until I hear it from him. Because there are exactly how many sides to every story? *Three.*

And *only a fool* will answer a matter before they hear it.

When someone comes to me wanting counseling, and doesn't bring their significant other or their spouse, I'll say, "I'm not doing that!" Why should we sit down and have a conversation that I know will involve another person when that person won't be there to speak for himself or herself? You're wasting my time *and* yours.

Why? Because only a fool answers the matter before they hear it.

Why? Because there are *three* sides—there's his side, there's her side, and then there's God's side.

Guess who's side *I'm* on!

So who do I need to hear from? I need to hear from her, I need to hear from him, and I need to hear from God. *Only a fool will answer a matter without hearing it.*

We don't go down the road of conjecture; we don't go down the road of listening to what only one person says. Do you have any idea how many people have been made shipwreck? That's why the Bible says a person who meddles in someone else's affairs is like a person who grabs a dog by the ears.

Do you know how many times somebody will come tell me something and I'll go straight to the person that they're talking about, and I'll say "I heard such-and-such, what happened?"

And they'll say, "Pastor, that didn't happen. Okay so, y'know what, Pastor? That *did* happen, but it wasn't quite *that* way—it was more like *this*."

"Oh, okay!"

Why jump to a conclusion when you can confront somebody and say, "This is what I heard, and I don't know if it's true or not true, but I'm not going to jump to a conclusion until I've heard it"?

See, so many people are *just immature* when it comes to realizing that they don't have all the answers.

Patience!

Understanding!

God uses weak things to confound the wise. He doesn't do everything the way *you* think it should be done. Listen, if *I* was God—and I'm not, but if I was—and I wanted to bring *my* child into this world, I would not allow a whore to be in the lineage. I just wouldn't have done that. I would've picked upstanding, contributing, non-back-laying individuals to be in the lineage of my holy child!

You'd better learn how not to be so judgmental about every single thing!

Now, if it's *doctrine*—we hold to that. You know I'm a stickler for doctrine; I'm not gonna change *anything* when it comes to doctrine. But people have added their own interpretations to *a lot of areas,* and I'm just not going to get in the middle of those things.

Years ago, my pastor told me that some situations are like flinging doo-doo. *Nobody wins.* 'Cause you've gotta touch it to throw it, and if somebody's throwing it at you? It's a mess. So no matter how you shake that up, you come out on the bad end of it.

This is why you've got to be very careful not to indict people or their situations, or to rail against people when you just don't know what they're going through.

I'll give you an example. I never liked the taste of alcohol. Never. I just have never liked the taste of it. So when I did drink, I was one of those frou-frou drink people—it had to be more of *everything else,* because I just didn't like the taste of it. So obviously, alcohol won't be the area Satan uses to attack me. Now, *chocolate cake,* on the other hand—that poses a *whole different problem!*

What I want you to understand is whatever you think when you judge somebody else and what they're going through, and you're like "I would never have done that, I would never do that, I would never be this, I would never, I would *never* …" until chocolate cake shows up!

See, Satan never uses *anything* against a person that does not have some level of enticement or draw.

If your struggle is women, *that's* what Satan's going to use.

If your struggle is money, *that's* what Satan's going to use.

If your struggle is possessions and things, *that's* what Satan is going to use.

If your struggle is drugs, *that's* what Satan is going to use.

Whatever it is that pushes your individual button is what Satan is going to use to mess you up. It's funny because every good and perfect gift comes from above, right? And the more perfect the gift is, the more challenging it is to God. It's interesting how God gave Eve to Adam; she directly assaulted Adam's relationship with God. Every good and *perfect* gift comes from above.

You mean to tell me that God can give you things *to see what you'll do with them*? To know what's in your heart?

"Will you choose alcohol over Me? Will you choose womanizing over Me? Will you choose stuff over Me?"

It goes right back to where we started. He said, "You honored your sons over Me."

Did you ever notice how Job corrected his children and made offerings for his children? Job was not gonna let them little midgets get away with anything! But why is that? *Because he honored God more.*

And God gave him double!

You've got to see the difference honoring God makes, because when you're dishonorable toward God, if I have to keep having a conversation with you about the basics—giving, serving, attending—if I've got to talk to you about those foundations of living out your faith, don't say anything about anybody. You just keep your mouth shut.

It's funny how husbands will talk about their wives; wives will talk about their husbands, kids will talk about their parents, parents will talk about their kids. They're learning from *you*!

You don't have any honor, and you wonder why they don't!

I'm not going to bring indictment against anybody. Listen, you do what you've got to do! I'm going to teach you what's right. I'm going to show you what it is. You're going to know; you're not going to get to heaven and be like, "I didn't know what honor was! You see, Lord, what happened was—I thought he was kidding!"

Nope. Mm-mm, I'm gonna do my job! My job is to share the truth with you.

I'm the FedEx guy. I bring the package, drop it off.

What you do with it from that point forward is up to you.

Remember what Paul said: "Things that are foolish to you? *God uses those* to confound people who think they're wise."[23]

Years ago, I had to go through a very public situation in our ministry—a divorce in the pulpit.

I had pastors call me and say, "So what are you going to do with your ministry?"

I said, "What do you mean, what am I going to do with it?"

"Well, you've got to shut it down!"

I said, "Okay, first of all—I went to all the leaders in the church and said, 'I wanna go'. And they said, 'If you go, we go,' so I didn't go. And I talked to *my* spiritual father, who was involved in this whole thing from the beginning, and he told me, 'We're not giving up on The Call!' So guess what we're doing?"

I had people call and tell me, "You're not going to make it; *nobody* makes it through that!"

One of the *specific* people, who *emphatically* told me I was not going to make it—*their* church is not around today. Careful what you put your mouth on.

---

[23] 1 Corinthians 1:27.

I wouldn't have chosen to go through it; I didn't want to go through it; didn't like it—still don't like it. But I can tell you this much: it had to be. And God protected me, and He kept me through it, and He blessed me through it. And so you can say what you want to say, but this is who I was, and this is who I am now, and God made the difference. I have nothing to say about people when they have to go through a struggle. And maybe I might be a little more merciful than I should!

"Well, Pastor, you know what they did, right?" *Yes.* I know what they did.

1 CORINTHIANS 14:26–33
How is it then, brethren? when ye come together, every one of you hath a psalm, hath a doctrine, hath a tongue, hath a revelation, hath an interpretation. Let all things be done unto edifying. If any man speak in an unknown tongue, let it be by two, or at the most by three, and that by course; and let one interpret. But if there be no interpreter, let him keep silence in the church; and let him speak to himself, and to God. Let the prophets speak two or three, and let the other judge. If any thing be revealed to another that sitteth by, let the first hold his peace. For ye may all prophesy one by one, that all may learn, and all may be comforted. And the spirits of the prophets are subject to the prophets. For God is not the author of confusion, but of peace, as in all churches of the saints.

"Brethren" means what? It means *you.* When you come together, *everybody* has a prophetic insight (or pathetic insight!), *everybody*'s got a gift, *everybody*'s got a tongue, *everybody*'s got something to say, but w*hatever it is,* let everything be instructive and for the good of all.

GALATIANS 6:1–2
Brethren, if a man be overtaken in a fault, ye which are spiritual, restore such an one in the spirit of

meekness; considering thyself, lest thou also be tempted. Bear ye one another's burdens, and so fulfil the law of Christ.

This scripture says, in other words, *it's a sign of immaturity when you want to indict what you should be restoring.* If you're immature and you see somebody who is struggling with—let's say with alcohol—and *you* struggle with alcohol? Don't go running into the bar trying to help them and save them!

You can't help me if you don't have victory over that which attacks me. That's why He said those that are godly, or spiritual, or mature, *those* are the ones to help restore.

It is *not my job* to run around as the Holy Ghost Police, reporting everything that everybody does wrong. Dear God, if I did that, I'd have nothing else to do! I don't agree with everybody and everything; *I don't have to.* I agree with the Bible, and I agree with the Word. And as long as the Word is the center of *my life*, then I'm responsible for driving *this* boat.

Now, everything under my responsibility, I have the right to deal with and judge—because guess who that includes? *All the members of my congregation!*

So what we do in my church, I have thoughts about! But everything outside of that? *Keep on keepin' on.* Hope that works out for you. I'm going to believe God with you—and if it doesn't work, we're always here to help!

Sometimes people come to me who have been dealing with different attacks in their life. If I don't recognize them as part of my flock, the first question I ask them is, "Am I your pastor?"

Now, this will catch people off-guard! They're like, "You're not gonna lay hands on me unless I tell you?"

No, I'm going to come into agreement with *you*. But now, you're working on *your* faith, not mine.

The centurion came to Jesus and said, "Lord, my servant is sick."

Jesus said, "I'll come to your house."

The centurion said, "No, you don't have to do that. Look, all you have to do is speak the Word."

The Bible says Jesus marveled at this.[24]

Do you believe Jesus *is, and was, and will always be God*?

Yes? Okay. So then, can you imagine something that made *God* marvel?

He made heaven and earth and all that is in them in *six days*, rested on the seventh not because he *needed* to but because He wanted to show *you* how to have some sense! And I can't get into an argument with you about Sabbath and taking a day off, I just can't even do it—I don't have the strength! If you don't have a Sabbath, you need to check yourself, because that's something you should have!

But anyway, He's *marveling*.

He's like, "*Wow!* Look at *this* guy! He says I don't even *have* to come to his house; all I've got to do is speak the Word *only!*"

The centurion explained, "The reason why is because I am a man under authority, and I have people under me. If I tell them to go, they go. If I tell them to sit, they sit. If I tell them to stand, they stand. I understand authority. It doesn't matter where I am when I tell them— as long as I say it, that's what is supposed to happen. So you don't even have to come to my house."

And Jesus was like, "Wow! *This guy*—look at *this guy* right here!"

That centurion understood some things!

---

24 Matthew 8:5-13; Luke 7:1-10.

I'm telling you, it would do us well to get clear about some things. That's why the Bible says there are silly women who run around looking for counseling in every which way they can, and never come to the truth. And trust me, there are just as many silly men who do the same thing! Wanting counseling from every direction, already have their answer, but can't hear it. Never coming to the truth. They just can't!

It's not my job.

God is God.

I have an assignment that focuses everything. Because some things that you're trying to fix are really just there to break your focus. Some of these axes that you keep grinding are just a waste of your time. You're just wasting time! Satan's the one telling you your ax is not sharp enough.

We are not to be indicting of other people; we are to be honorable.

You want to show somebody how it's done? Show them how it's done.

You've got something to say about it? Then you be different. *Be the change* that you so proclaim you want to see, and let *your life* be the platform or the stage on which other people see what is right.

Some ministers have so disrespected me—I still love on them; I've given them offerings; I've been a blessing to them when they've been *very* disrespectful to me. But that *does not change my honor*. It doesn't change who I am. I don't care how you deal with me. I may not give you access anymore, but I'm not going to be running around talking smack.

I've had people try to destroy *my* name in the event that I would retaliate for what *they* did to me!

But when you're honorable? God will raise you up out of that nonsense.

When you're honorable, God will fight for you.
Isn't that something?

CHAPTER 5

IGNORING

The concept of honor is definitely lost—not just in the world! Unfortunately, there's a point where the church begins to imitate the world, and I mean "church" universally. We have to be very careful about honor, because God responds to honor. Believe it or not, honor is one of the currencies of heaven! Your money doesn't mean anything if you're not honorable with it.

Let's go back to 1 Samuel 2:29–36:

> **Wherefore kick ye at my sacrifice and at mine offering, which I have commanded in my habitation; and honourest thy sons above me, to make yourselves fat with the chiefest of all the offerings of Israel my people? Wherefore the LORD God of Israel saith, I said indeed that thy house, and the house of thy father, should walk before me for ever: but now the LORD saith, Be it far from me; for them that honour me I will honour, and they that despise me shall be lightly esteemed. Behold, the days come that I will cut off thine arm, and the arm of thy father's house, that there shall not be an old man in thine house. And thou shalt see an enemy in my habitation, in all the wealthy which God shall give Israel: and there shall not be an old man in thine house for ever. And the man of thine, whom I shall not cut off from mine altar, shall be to consume thine eyes, and to grieve thine heart: and all the**

increase of thine house shall die in the flower of their age. And this shall be a sign unto thee, that shall come upon thy two sons, on Hophni and Phinehas; in one day they shall die both of them. And I will raise me up a faithful priest, that shall do according to that which is in mine heart and in my mind: and I will build him a sure house; and he shall walk before mine anointed for ever. And it shall come to pass, that every one that is left in thine house shall come and crouch to him for a piece of silver and a morsel of bread, and shall say, Put me, I pray thee, into one of the priests' offices, that I may eat a piece of bread.

It's interesting that God had said they were going to walk before Him forever, and then He said, "You know what? But not anymore." I don't necessarily believe God changed His mind about them as much as I believe that the more dishonorable a person is, the harder it is for God to function and operate. Because the currency of heaven is honor.

Remember that He said, "You put your sons before Me; you put your children before Me; you put other things in My place—so that means you have lightly esteemed Me. Because you lightly esteemed Me, I am lightly esteeming you."

I think the promise God gave them was that they would be held in high regard and high esteem. But it was predicated upon them holding God in high regard and high esteem. Now, this priest Eli's children did some really crazy stuff! For one thing, they were having sex with goddesses and women in God's tabernacle (and how many of you know, that doesn't even make any kind of sense!) That's the type of stuff they were doing!

God is like, "You honored your kids above Me, because you *allowed* them to do these things. You allowed them to function with such disregard. You allowed them to be unfaithful."

Notice something: *Unfaithfulness is a dishonor.*

God said, "What I'm going to do is I'm going to raise Me up a *faithful* priest."

So then what God attributed to dishonor was *unfaithfulness*.

And He said, "If you esteem Me, I'll esteem you. If you honor Me, I'll honor you. If you lightly esteem Me, then I will lightly esteem you."

So many people put everything else before God. This is a very difficult kind of conversation, if you will. Think about how people will put their job before church; they'll put their children before church; they will put their family before their commitments to God.

I'll give you an example. Our church had an initial meeting for our security team, and many people showed up that weren't faithful! We had a lot of faithful folks, don't get me wrong, but we also had people who were *not* faithful yet showed up wanting to protect us. *You have to be here!*

Are you going to send the Ghost of Christmas Past?

Think about it for a second! People don't realize how dishonorable and unfaithful they are, how disrespectfully they handle the things of God.

It's been written that people would come to Smith Wigglesworth's house to be ministered to—if you don't know who he is, look him up! His wife would seat them, and he would go and change into a suit and tie—and *then* he would come down and minister to them—that was his value and honor for his office as a minister. Now, he didn't sit around on his couch in a suit and tie, but when the ministry came calling, or when the request or demand was placed, he had such honor for God's gifting that he said, "I won't even execute the offices or the function of my office until I have donned a better attire."

How do we descend from *that level* of honor to where people think it doesn't matter how they handle things, how they handle a man or woman of God, how they handle their pastors, how they handle their ministry leaders, how they handle one another, how they handle the things of God?

How do we process what that means?

Say, for example, your church hosts an event and struggles to get people even to *support* the event. Your church has a movie night, gives away free food, but *still* can't get people to support it.

What you value and what you find weighty will always show up in what you choose to do and not to do. So it's amazing to me when our church has a work day, how many people don't show up. Don't get me wrong, because lots of people do show up for work day! At one time, no one showed up but me and three other people! I'm grateful for all those who *do* show up and help on work day—but what amazes me is how many people *don't* show up. And it's their house! It's not like they're being asked to clean another church, or take care of another church, it's *their church*! It's *their* house!

People are always in a process of development.

The first thing they always say is "Pastor, it's *your* church." Then they tend to say "*our* church." And eventually, through the progression of time, they'll begin to say "*my* church."

I'm always looking for people to say "*my* church," because that means they've taken ownership, just like I have, of that which truly belongs to God, but it displays personal ownership. And when you value and you give weight to things, that's honoring.

Remember the Scales of Justice? How when you put more weights on one side, the heavier side tips downward and the lighter side goes up? That word, honor, means to apply weight to it or to add more pounds to it in order to make it weightier, or to make it heavier.

If you were to make a list of the most prosperous people in our church, of those who are the lenders and not the borrowers, I would be able to show you their level of honor. Literally! I could show you the extent and the level of the honor they have toward the things of God, toward me as their leader, toward the people of our church and its organization as a whole—I'd be able to break it down for you.

Yet those who struggle never seem to be able to connect the dots that their struggle is because of their lack of honor. This is why this is such a huge issue! Because I really do believe that if we get this straight, it will change *so much* in our lives.

This chapter's "I" is IGNORING.

GENESIS 3:1–7
Now the serpent was more subtil than any beast of the field which the LORD God had made. And he said unto the woman, Yea, hath God said, Ye shall not eat of every tree of the garden? And the woman said unto the serpent, We may eat of the fruit of the trees of the garden: But of the fruit of the tree which is in the midst of the garden, God hath said, Ye shall not eat of it, neither shall ye touch it, lest ye die. And the serpent said unto the woman, Ye shall not surely die: For God doth know that in the day ye eat thereof, then your eyes shall be opened, and ye shall be as gods, knowing good and evil. And when the woman saw that the tree was good for food, and that it was pleasant to the eyes, and a tree to be desired to make one wise, she took of the fruit thereof, and did eat, and gave also unto her husband with her; and he did eat. And the eyes of them both were opened, and they knew that they were naked; and they sewed fig leaves together, and made themselves aprons.

Here's a question for you: Did Eve know not to do it? *Yes.*

Was she told by God directly? *No.*

So who told her? *Adam.*

Because who did God tell? *Adam.*

So here God told *Adam*—but didn't even tell *her*. Adam then told her what God said. She was aware of what God said. So then by IGNORING the preacher, Adam, who told her, she ignored *God*. So now here she is, because Satan's working on her now, she eats the fruit.

And then *this* knucklehead, Adam, eats it! *He* ignored God *directly*!

Did he know better? *Yes.*

Was he told better? *Yes.*

God really expects you to walk in the light you have. And I think one of the greatest challenges people have is that they *know* better, but they can't seem to muster the faith it takes to *do* better, and the execution that it takes to function. Now, I don't know why this is, because when I hear things in the Bible, I automatically assume it's talking to me! I really do. I don't care what it is, I don't care what it says, I *automatically assume* that it's talking to me. Now, obviously, I am not perfect, but I'm always thrown by people who can hear a Word preached to them and *totally ignore* what was said. They just tune it out as if you never said it.

My wife and I will joke sometimes because we'll preach something and—it never fails—maybe a day or two days later, somebody will do *exactly the opposite* of what we *know* we just preached. And I'm thinking to myself, "Were they there?" And ultimately, I'll find out they were!

And then I'll say, "Was I stuck on 'Ignore'? Did they put me on DND, 'Do Not Disturb'?"

You have to ask yourself some of these tough questions, because it's dishonorable to God to put Him on "Ignore." And we see very clearly in our passage from Genesis—*they were told!*

But yet they still ate the fruit.

GENESIS 3:7–11
And the eyes of them both were opened, and they knew that they were naked; and they sewed fig leaves together, and made themselves aprons. And they heard the voice of the LORD God walking in the garden in the cool of the day: and Adam and his wife hid themselves from the presence of the LORD God amongst the trees of the garden. And the LORD God called unto Adam, and said unto him, Where art thou? And he said, I heard thy voice in the garden, and I was afraid, because I was naked; and I hid myself. And he said, Who told thee that thou wast naked? Has thou eaten of the tree, whereof I commanded thee that thou shouldest not eat?

I know some of you like to dress up your pets—don't get mad at me!

I know some of you like to do that, and y'all think it's cute! But I can tell you this much: Your dog does not care whether it's naked or not! There's nothing in your dog that says, "I need a certain type of jeans, and I need a certain outfit, and if it ain't this, then I don't wanna wear it!" There is absolutely *zero shame*. A dog will pee wherever it wants, no shame!

It's amazing to me how *we* were designed that way. Because God asks—He says, *"Who told you?* Where did you get this idea from that all of a sudden you have to cover up?" And so the perversion begins.

GENESIS 3:12
And the man said, The woman whom thou gavest to be with me, she gave me of the tree, and I did eat. And the LORD God said unto the woman, what is this that thou hast done? And the woman said, The serpent beguiled me, and I did eat.

Adam says, *"That woman* you gave me…." Typical man!

Instead of just saying "You know what, I messed up," he blames it on her. And you know the rest of the story.

Ignoring God when He tells you things is crazy because there's a reason for whatever He tells you! It's like when you tell somebody, "Don't be unequally yoked," and it goes in one ear and out the other. I can *literally count on one hand* how many people have truly avoided being unequally yoked in my fourteen years of ministry. *Fourteen years* of ministry, and I can count on one hand how many people I've seen successfully negotiate not becoming unequally yoked—isn't that crazy? You know why? *Because they're stuck on "Ignore."*

One of the most dangerous things people will do is choose not to go to marriage counseling. (I won't officiate a wedding without marriage counseling, because I don't do funerals!) Okay, yes, I do funerals, but I don't do *funerals*—not that kind of funeral! I'm not going to do a wedding that's going to turn into a metaphorical funeral. Do you understand what I'm saying?

So they'll void all of that opportunity to get premarital wisdom and insight, because they're like, "I don't want to submit myself to that process." You know what that process is designed to do? *Make sure you're not unequally yoked.* Because "equally yoked" doesn't just mean that you're yoked to someone who professes to be a believer; "equally yoked" means that you are connected with someone who is going the same way you're going.

In other words, if you're married to somebody and they're not in church like you are? They're not serving like you are? *You're unequally yoked.* The truth of the matter is one will pull the other out! And guess what usually happens? It's never the one who's serving God who pulls the other one in. What tends to happen is the one who's on the outside will go to church just long enough to snatch who it is they're interested in!

It never ceases to amaze me how sex, soul ties, and emotions will cause people to defy the "unequally yoked" rule.

"Well, we've already done this, we've already crossed this bridge, we've already gotten to this place, so we might as well go on ahead and get married." The next thing you know, she's pregnant, and everybody's doing the math!

ROMANS 1:18
For the wrath of God is revealed from heaven against all ungodliness and unrighteousness of men, who hold the truth in unrighteousness."

Notice what the apostle Paul is saying here: He says the wrath of God is not against *you*!

So I'm telling you that if you suppress the truth, if you act like it doesn't exist, if you *ignore what you know is better*—because some people think if they can just suppress it and act like it doesn't happen —you're engaging in what I call The Ostrich Effect. If you bury your head in the ground, you don't see the lion coming anymore, so you think you're not going to die. But I assure you, the lion is not going to stop and go, "Ohhh, snap! They buried their head in the ground! Guess I can't eat 'em now!" No, that lion is still coming, and you're still going to end up as his lunch! *Putting it under the rug is not the same as putting it under the blood.*

ROMANS 1:19–21
Because that which may be known of God is manifest in them; for God hath showed it unto them. For the invisible things of him from the creation of the world are clearly seen, being understood by the things that are made, even his eternal power and Godhead; so that they are without excuse: Because that, when they knew God, they glorified him not as God, neither were thankful; but became vain in their imaginations, and their foolish heart was darkened.

So, in other words, there's no excuse!

I knew a very, *very* popular minister, one of the first people to have *thousands* in a megachurch. If a church has more than 2,000 people, it's considered a megachurch. If a church has more than 200 people, believe it or not, it's considered a large church because 80% of all churches are fewer than 100 people. A lot of people don't know that!

Anyway, this particular minister had *thousands*, and his father passed away. When that happened, the problem he was trying to reconcile is that he was not convinced, because of his father's lifestyle, that his father was saved. It had always been this pastor's desire to *lead* his father to the Lord—it just never manifested. So he began to teach a doctrine that there was no hell. It started out slowly, because in *his* mind, he could not accept the fact that if his father was not saved, was not in heaven, but in hell.

It caused him to redefine his doctrine.

The next thing you know, this pastor was labeled as a heretic. His church is now nowhere close to what it used to be. And then he moved into universalism—that's the new-age stuff—and it's been downhill ever since.

Now, who am I to judge another man's servant? But I want you to understand the story; I want you to understand the point I'm making. The point is: *When God is revealed, you cannot change it because of how* you *feel.*

And you have to be very careful that you don't allow yourself—because you can't seem to get *your* head wrapped around it—to begin to refute or *negate* the things which have already been clearly stated.

Our Romans passage says "although they *knew* God...." I cannot tell you how many people can quote scripture, and can be as legalistic as they want to be, and they can come up with all kinds of stuff that is legalistic in their minds, and in their thinking, they *know* God—but if they *know* God, then God's precepts should be higher than theirs, and they should *honor God as God.*

Not as "You know, this is just a cool guy who's got a book."

So the pastor I mentioned above said, "I used to believe that the Word of God was, in fact, the Word of God inspired through man. But what I began to realize was that the Bible is the inspired word of man, *about* God."

Our passage says that *"although they knew God...."* In order for you to really know God *as God,* you have to *honor* God. And in order to honor God, you have to *follow* God—not *your* precepts *of* God— and allow Him to *be* God over all areas of your life. So if you struggle in the area of finances, and you know what God says about it, *you're ignoring God.* You'd be better off just being obedient than to be ignoring Him!

Let's go back to the whole "unequally yoked" thing.

I cannot tell you how many times my wife and I have sat through counseling sessions with people whom we *know* are unequally yoked. And we believe *they* know they're unequally yoked! What we have wracked our brains trying to figure out is *why. We* know it; we believe *they* know it!

"For although they knew God, they did not honor Him as God, or give thanks to Him."

Notice something: Not honoring God includes not giving thanks to God. He said they didn't *honor* God, which means they didn't listen and apply what they knew, *and* they didn't give thanks, but they became futile!

Do you know what "futile" is? *Useless.*

It means "produces no result." It means "destitute of power." *Futile.*

Do you ever wonder why certain things in your life feel like they're just futile? Like they're not working? Like things don't seem to have the power that they should? You watch other people and you're like, "They seem to operate with the power of God, but I don't know why I can't seem to get it."

How honorable are you toward the things of God? How weighty are they?

Do you say you're going to serve and then don't show up? You know God says to give your best to Him! You'll show up at work on time. Your boss will call a meeting, and you're there! Your ministry leader will call a meeting, and you've got 50 million other things you've got to do. *No honor.*

It's not weighty anymore.

Going back to Romans, they were darkened because of *futility* in their thinking and their foolish hearts. But to be darkened means *they had light.*

It's *your* job to keep the lights on. It's *your* job to not allow foolishness.

ROMANS 1:22–23
Professing themselves to be wise, they became fools, and changed the glory of the uncorruptible God into an image made like to corruptible man, and to birds, and fourfooted beasts, and creeping things.

Do you have any idea how most people think who defy the things of God that they're ignoring—if you want to be honest? Nobody defies and ignores God saying, "Oh, I'm just ignoring God!"

What they have is a logic that creeps in, and the logic begins to *explain away.*

"Well, I know God said that, but He wasn't talking to *me* because in *my* situation, my heart is different! God knows my heart!"

You know, the Bible says that if you are operating in delusion, God will give you over to your lie. You believe it so much that you'll defy everything that God has said—God will *give you over to it* and allow you to have it. Because evidently you want it so badly!

It doesn't change that He won't bless it.

Back in 1 Samuel, God said, "You honored your sons above Me. Now what I told you was going to happen is not going to happen. *I'm giving you over to this.*"

And then people cry, "God, get me out of this! God, deliver me from this relationship! Pastor, I don't know what went wrong!"

I do. You decided what *you* were going to do, and you *ignored God*. And because you gave no honor to God, God brought no honor upon you.

Do you ever stop and think that sometimes the things God asks you to do are *actually for your benefit*? Is that not a foreign concept?

Most people are like, "Well, God just doesn't want me to have fun."

Do you ever think that some of the things God asks you to do, asks you to give up or walk away from, asks you to let go of, that He *actually does it for your sake?* For your own good?

Or He can just give you over to what you want, because you want it.

Whenever things in someone's life begin to come against God, and their *true desire* is to come against God, against *what they know*—this ain't Old Testament; this is the book of Romans! Paul is saying this is true in *this dispensation*—that people are just given over to it. He said that for this reason, God gave them up to dishonorable passions, and they received in themselves the penalties of their errors.

"Pastor, are you trying to tell me that if I'm so dishonorable, I can literally create my own penalties that I keep trying to pray away? I'm praying, and I'm rubbing people's heads until their hair is *smooth off their head*! You mean to tell me that the problem could be *me?* That dishonor is such a stronghold in me that I *have* to believe it?"

I've seen people post things about doing what the Word says and not being selective, and then they don't go to church.

I say, "Wait a minute, what about what the Word tells *you* to do?"

You do know that the Word says, "Go to church," right? The Bible says, "*Forsake not the assembling of yourselves together.*"[25] The word "assembly" here is the word for "temple" or "building," a variation of "synagogue." So it means "Come to the building," or "Come to the house of God for worship."

And it says don't act like people toward the *end* of times, where they'll ignore it and not do it because they've got other reasons—that's what the Bible says! So if that's what the Bible says, tell me why you have to have something in your head that convinces you otherwise.

It isn't a demon, it's a stronghold!

HOSEA 4:6
My people are destroyed for lack of knowledge: because thou hast rejected knowledge, I will also reject thee, that thou shalt be no priest to me: seeing thou hast forgotten the law of thy God, I will also forget thy children.

The implication here is that the people don't know. Right? *Lack of knowledge.*

In other words, there's a difference between being ignorant and being stupid!

Ignorant means you don't know. *Stupid* is when you know, but you do it anyway.

Here's the problem: He says the reason they have a lack of knowledge is because they have *rejected* knowledge. So that means they're not ignorant! It isn't that they don't know. They can't sit there and say, "Oh well, y'know, I just didn't know, so that's my excuse."

So how does someone know if they're unequally yoked? If they're with somebody who knows better but acts stupid, they're not ignorant!

---

[25] Hebrews 10:25.

MALACHI 2:5–9
My covenant was with him of life and peace; and I
gave them to him for the fear wherewith he feared
me, and was afraid before my name. The law of
truth was in his mouth, and iniquity was not found
in his lips: he walked with me in peace and equity,
and did turn many away from iniquity. For the
priest's lips should keep knowledge, and they should
seek the law at his mouth: for he is the messenger of
the LORD of hosts. But ye are departed out of the
way; ye have caused many to stumble at the law; ye
have corrupted the covenant of Levi, saith the LORD
of hosts. Therefore have I also made you
contemptible and base before all the people,
according as ye have not kept my ways, but have
been partial in the law.

Has there ever been any perfect person to walk the planet other than Jesus? *No.*

So then He *cannot* be talking about perfection in this verse. He *cannot* be saying, "You kept all of the law, so that's why I blessed you." What He said was, "Your problem was that you were *partial.*"

"Partial" means that you have *preferences* and predilections as to how you *apply* what you know. In other words, you come to the Bible as if it's a smorgasbord! And since you don't like the peas, you'll just ignore that part, right?

I hate peas to this day. I really do. The other day, my wife took some peas out of the freezer and put them in the refrigerator. I opened the refrigerator and saw a bag of peas, and I threw 'em down the hallway! Truth! *I hate peas.* Just hate them. And if any of you try to be a prankster and bring me some peas, I'm gonna throw them at you!

So my wife was trying to convince me about peas and how good they are, and said, "Then *you* eat them! But I made a decision when I was a little kid that when I got grown, I was *not* gonna eat any peas!"

Now, I *do* like the crunchy wasabi peas. But the *mushy ones*?

You know how people say, "You go together like peas and carrots"? *That is not a compliment!*

When I was a kid, my mom put peas on my plate, and my mom didn't cook five dinners every night! She cooked one, and you ate what was in front of you! Nowadays, I hear parents say, "I made this one for So-and-so because they have an allergy to this, and I made this one for this person because they don't like this." Yeah, allergy or no allergy, we had one dinner and you were gonna eat it!

So I started feeding the peas to the dog. One by one, he was grubbing 'em!

I thought, "Let me just go on ahead and pour these in his bowl with his dog food, and he'll eat them!"

You know that stupid dog wouldn't eat them once they got in his bowl!

So now I'm thinking to myself, "My mom might just come in here and make me pick those peas out of that dog food!"

I had three brothers—my mom raised *four boys.* She was stone cold!

So I'm there thinking, "I'm gonna have to eat dog food *and* peas!"

Long story short, my mom came in and saw the peas, and she dished me out a new helping of peas, and then let me sit there until I ate them all. So in that traumatic situation, I decided that once I got grown enough to determine what it is I'm going to eat, I ain't eatin' no peas!

Now that's my predilection. Some of you may like peas!

Now, if the Bible said, "Thou shalt eat peas"? Then I'm going to have to learn how to like some peas! But since it doesn't, that's one of the things left to my discretion, and I can be partial.

But when it comes to the Word of God?

I am not allowed to behave as if God's Word is a smorgasbord where I pick the parts I want and reject the parts I don't. Malachi says the partiality was what God found dishonorable. It had nothing to do with them being imperfect; we're all imperfect! But He had a problem with hypocrisy.

That partiality created hypocrisy. And *that* was His issue.

Isn't that something?

JOHN 12:48
He that rejecteth me, and receiveth not my words, hath one that judgeth him: the word that I have spoken, the same shall judge him in the last day.

You know when people say "Don't judge me"?

You're better off with me judging you than you are when you refuse to judge yourself for something. He said if you *don't* deal with it, then you do have a judge! And your judge is not your *perception* of the Word I spoke. Your judge is not what you *thought* I said. What will judge you is, in fact, *what you rejected.* It's what you're not hearing. It's what you're not listening to.

You want to prosper, but you don't want to give—you've rejected it, so then you'll never prosper.

That behavior will judge you.

You want things, you want situations to change, you want to be healed, you want certain things to happen—but you reject God's Word, so it judges you.

And you run around saying, "Don't judge me!" *I'm not!*

The Word's doing a real good job of it!

JAMES 1:19-22
Wherefore, my beloved brethren, let every man be

swift to hear, slow to speak, slow to wrath: For the wrath of man worketh not the righteousness of God. Wherefore lay apart all filthiness and superfluity of naughtiness, and receive with meekness the engrafted word, which is able to save your souls. But be ye doers of the word, and not hearers only, deceiving your own selves. But be ye doers of the word, and not hearers only, deceiving your own selves. For if any be a hearer of the word, and not a doer, he is like unto a man beholding his natural face in a glass: For he beholdeth himself, and goeth his way, and straightway forgetteth what manner of man he was. But whoso looketh into the perfect law of liberty, and continueth therein, he being not a forgetful hearer, but a doer of the work, this man shall be blessed in his deed.

Who is James talking to here? *The church.*

When you hear "Brethren," he's talking to *you* as church folk, right?

Notice what he says—if you are *hearers* of the Word—you've heard it, but you just refuse to do it. And ultimately, the only person you have deceived is yourself. He's telling you, "Don't deceive yourself!" Allow the Word to become engrafted.

He says those that are a *hearer* of the Word, but not a *doer* of the Word, are like a man who looks in a mirror. He looks at himself, gets himself dressed up, gets his hair just right, beard all shaped up, and everything is the way it needs to be. He looks at himself in the mirror, and then he walks away and *forgets* what manner of man he is.

So you mean to tell me that if I'm a *doer* of the Word, everything I do will be blessed as long as I don't forget? As long as I don't ignore what manner of person I really am from what the Word says, and not from my personal predilections?

Are you telling me that if I'm not a doer of the Word, there's a possibility that the things I do are *not* blessed because I really don't know the engrafted Word?

When I teach messages like this, people might begin to think, "Well, Pastor, this is very oppressing. This is very restrictive! I just don't believe God is that way. I want to be free! I want to have liberty!" Notice what the Bible calls "liberty": *It's to continue in what God has said.*

In other words, with the Word of God comes *real* freedom.

"I just don't do organized church, because I want to be free!" *Dummy.* Nothing's "free" about that. Nothing's "free" about living for the world; you *will* pay!

Most people know when they're doing stuff that's wrong. They know they're wrong; it's not ignorance! They're just *ignoring* it. Sweeping it under the rug, acting like it didn't happen, acting like it wasn't said.

He said the man who continues to live in obedience to what God says shall be blessed in all that he does.

There are people who aspire to such a level of prosperity that they would not be a good Christian witness if they got there. There are people who *aspire*—they can talk the talk; they can act like they've got the faith language down; they've got champagne tastes, but a soda-pop budget, and Cracker Jack faith.

The truth is, the reason they're struggling is they're not honorable toward God. And if God *allowed* you to have what you desire to the level you desire it, you wouldn't be a good Christian witness! Do you see that?

Honor is everything.

Maybe you think you're a person who doesn't desire more—and if you say that, you're lying! That just doesn't make sense. Because nobody is satisfied with where they are right now. Everybody has in them the desire for more—God placed that in you!

If you're getting close to achieving all you've ever dreamed of, you don't have a God-sized dream! Because a God-sized dream should always be eluding you—*always*! Once you think you get there, you realize it's way bigger than you thought, it's further out there.

So think about this: If you want to be blessed in all you do, then God expects you to be honorable. And as you are honorable, as you represent Him, then you can be blessed in all your deeds—because you'll represent Him the in much the same way as you represented Him in the little.

If you make $2,000 a year and are able to tithe, when you make $200,000 a year you're still going to be able to tithe. When you make $2,000,000 dollars a year, you're *still* going to be able to tithe!

See, God knows us better than we think! And if we are going to be honorable toward His Word, then we will not ignore it. Your pastor may preach something that hits you right where you live! But honor will keep you from getting mad and storming out of the church.

You need to realize that the sign of sonship is *correction*. That's the sign of sonship!

And listen, if I can be the Bride of Christ, then ladies, you can be the Sons of God. So "sonship" means *fatherhood*, and correction is a sign of that relationship!

If you have *never* felt inside you that you could do better and you've missed the mark, that you need to bring yourself up and make some corrections—the Bible says you're a bastard!

And a bastard is a person without a father.

You have a daddy! And He desires for you to continue to come up! He says, "When you honor Me, I'll honor you." I don't know about you, but *I like to be honored!* So we have to learn how to keep honoring in awe.

THE EYES OF HONOR: THE CURRENCY OF HEAVEN

CHAPTER 6

INDISCRETION

Our first text for this chapter is 2 Samuel 11:1:

And it came to pass, after the year was expired, at the time when kings go forth to battle, that David sent Joab, and his servants with him, and all Israel; and they destroyed the children of Ammon, and besieged Rabbah. But David tarried still at Jerusalem.

This honor message has been stirring inside me because, I'm telling you, honor is one of the major problems affecting the Body of Christ.

I was watching a movie where an attorney was speaking to a bunch of young people, and one of the ladies was standing, so he challenged a young man to give up his seat so she could sit down. And she took great offense to that. She said, "I'm a woman, I can stand just like any man can."

I think one of the challenges in our society is that it's not a matter of whether or not a woman can do what a man can do; it's a matter of honor. And chivalry is really dead. It's been killed not only by men, but by women as well. Somehow the interpretation of that which is ancient has been interpreted as outdated, and the truth of the matter is that just because it's ancient doesn't mean it's outdated. It doesn't mean there's something wrong with it.

If you're sitting somewhere and you see an older person coming, you should offer your seat. But that's not the norm anymore. Kids nowadays will look at you like you lost your mind! And the nature of honor, the nature of understanding honor, the nature of discerning honor is significant because honorable people handle themselves differently than dishonorable people do. And I don't know if it's just a matter of kids not being taught what is honorable anymore; I don't know exactly why honor is not as big a thing as it used to be. Some kids these days have no home training! They act like they've got no home whatsoever.

I think you have to begin to ask yourself—if Satan knows that honor is a very big thing to God, then if I were Satan and I had a plan to derail society, one of the first things I would do is take away honor. One of the first things I would do is begin to erode the necessity and the expectation of honor.

I've watched people in relationships, particularly women, who don't expect anything from a man. They don't expect him to open the door; they don't expect him to take care of the bill; they don't expect him to do what's right concerning them. And the Bible says there will come a time where there are seven women to one man, and they won't expect a thing from him! The Bible says that! It says there will be such a shortage of men that the standards women have will completely drop in order to get him to fit. The truth of the matter is that if you required and demanded respect, and if you demanded honor, then you would weed out a lot of people very, very quickly. And there's nothing wrong with weeding out people, because presence does not resolve loneliness; suitability does.

I've heard so many people complain, "This is not honorable! My husband, my boyfriend, my this or that, they're not honorable, they're not doing certain things!" And I think, "You never required them to do certain things! Your requirements changed after you got him, because you were too afraid to set the bar and say, 'Now you're going to have to jump over this.'"

The slow erosion of this place of honor has occurred. It has caused people to not even realize what honor really is. When you begin to say, "I love God," know that there are a lot of people who love God, but don't honor God. It's like when someone says they love you, but they won't honor you. If they loved you, they would honor you! Because honor and love are not separate from each other. Honor is a place where you put someone and you esteem them above yourself.

How do you deal with the things of God? How do you deal with His things in your life?

At a time when David should have been off to war—he should have been carrying his army's banner—he's sitting on a rooftop looking at a woman who's bathing, who also happens to be someone else's wife!

Our society tends not to frown-upon a man having an affair, but it is frowned upon or looked at in a certain way when a woman has an affair. Yet the truth is that the statistics are almost identical in terms of the number of women who cheat on their husbands versus the number of husbands who cheat on their wives today. It wasn't that way thirty years ago, but the numbers are evening out today. So now in our society, you see things happening—more and more women are moving out of the fidelity of their relationships. It happens so often, and I don't know if it's life imitating art, or art imitating life—but the problem is that dishonorable behavior is perpetuated by media. Anything you watch, you'll see it! It's so blatantly obvious. People are jumping from bed to bed, running from responsibility. You'll hear men saying, "I take care of my kids!" You don't get a prize from me because you take care of your kids! That's not even a discussion; we're not going to pat you on the head because you take care of your children! You're *supposed* to take care of your kids. You're supposed to take care of your wife!

But what happens is we begin to reward that which is dishonorable, and that's the point that I'm trying to make. We begin to advertise what is dishonorable, because you're not going to watch a soap opera about God! It's not going to capture your attention; you need some *juice*—you need something to happen that is so outlandish it'll capture your attention so all the advertisers can program you to buy the things they want you to buy.

One of my favorite TV shows was *Miami Vice*. Per season, there were 26 episodes—*26 episodes!* Nowadays you're lucky if a season has ten! And you're lucky (if it's an hour show) if you get thirty minutes of content because the other thirty minutes are commercials selling you stuff that you don't need! Y'all gotta wake up and see it, because society is being pushed in a direction where honor is no longer important and being honorable is no longer valued.

In biblical times, people *died* over honor! If you questioned their honor, if you called them on the carpet about their honor, people would put their life on the line to defend their honor!

Nowadays? It's not even important.

A lot of teaching about David and Bathsheba is billed as "the key scripture to teach your kids about sexual immorality." The truth of the matter is that David and Bathsheba have absolutely nothing to do with sexual immorality. Even later, God told him, "I gave you the wives of your king, and if that wasn't enough, all you had to do was ask Me and I'd have given you more."[26]

This episode had nothing to do with the sexual aspect of David and Bathsheba's relationship, and in fact it really had nothing to with David or Bathsheba! Even when you see the story referenced in the

---

[26] 2 Samuel 12:8.

New Testament, it calls Bathsheba the wife of Uriah. This story has everything to do with Uriah, and very little to do with the other cast of characters!

Here David brings this man home from war so he will sleep with his own wife in order to mess up the timeline of her pregnancy! Here David is working this plan—the Bible says he sends a whole mess of meat to his house and he says, "You're going to eat well and lay with your wife, and then my problems are over because now nobody's going to know that this baby you're about to raise is mine!" The deceptiveness of it! To a man who laid on his doorstep and said, "I'm not going to go home and enjoy the comforts of it when the ark sleeps in a tent, when the commander sleeps in a tent, when my Lord sleeps in a tent."

He could have said, "This is the come-up! The Lord is my shepherd, He knows what I want. Everybody else gets to sit out there in the freezing cold in a tent, and I get to go home and snuggle up next to my wife!"

Even in the presence of the temptation to do what's *legally right*— there's nothing wrong with him sleeping with his wife!—in his heart of hearts, his honor says, "I can't do that."

This chapter's "I" is INDISCRETION.

"Indiscretion" means not making good choices in situations you are presented with. When you are acting indiscreetly, you are absolutely blithely unaware of what's going on around you—what's appropriate, what isn't appropriate, what's the right thing to do, what's the wrong thing to do.

And so many people think, "Well, honor is an *internal* thing, it's how I feel." No, honor is how you act.

And love is a verb! So many people think love is a feeling, but love is not a feeling. If you're in high school or junior high, love can be a feeling for you because you can be Twitter-pated like a little high school kid. But when you grow up, you realize that love is not a feeling—love is a verb! It is what you *do;* it is based on commitment. As you begin to operate in a place of commitment, your feelings don't have much to do with it! If I'm committed to you, then I'm committed to you when you're not wearing makeup. I'm committed to you when your breath stinks. I'm committed to you when you wake up looking like a different person than I went to sleep with! That's commitment.

Honorable people do not change with the emotion of where they are and when they said things. It's like integrity. Integrity is following through with what you said even long after the mood you said it in has passed.

How many people have promised you things in the mood, in the moment, then when that moment passed they forgot all about it? It's just not important, it's not significant, and it's dishonorable.

So for this man Uriah to be mindful of where all his fellow soldiers are, the real issue in this story is how David deals with an honorable man! That's the real issue.

Here the New Testament speaks of this guy by name!

David killed his body, but God preserved his legacy.

How you deal with the things concerning God is important. You have to know it's significant that you have discretion about discerning things when it comes to the works of God, the people of God, the things of God.

PROVERBS 5:1
My son, attend unto my wisdom, and bow thine ear to my understanding: That thou mayest regard discretion, and that thy lips may keep knowledge.

I often have to deal with various relationship situations. Let's say there's a boyfriend and girlfriend—and the girlfriend is off the chain, and the boyfriend will come and say, "Well, I don't know what to do!"

And I'm like, "Well, first of all, you've got to get honest about what's going on."

And they say, "Well, you know, I just don't want to believe it."

This is a very serious problem! Especially with married people. When you're sleeping with the enemy, it's hard to see what the enemy's doing.

And when they come to me as a third party, I'll tell them flat-out "I don't see it the way you see it, because I'm not sleeping with them. I see it for what it is. This is a problem. This is evil and you're gonna have to deal with it!"

Most people don't want to deal with it. Their ability to see and discern will change their level of being honorable, because they're yoked into a situation they don't want to see for what it really is.

That's why Proverbs says, "You bow your ear to the Word. You bow your ear to what is right. It doesn't matter if the king calls you in from war and sends you home with a mess of meat when you know the rest of your squad is out there in the cold, suffering. You don't get to enjoy what you want to enjoy if you're an honorable person. Your honor does not change because of other people."

If you're not careful, you'll become afraid to hold what's honorable in the face of the pressure imposed by people who are dishonorable! It'll mess with your emotions; it'll mess with your feelings; it'll mess with your conscience; and it'll cause you to enter a place where you cannot even see up from down, or "come here" from "sic 'em." This is why having discretion—your ability to see a situation for what it really is, even if you're in it—then making a stand for God is so important.

I've observed people dealing with a spouse who doesn't want to be involved in church or the things of God. These unequally yoked people get hot and heavy for God; they get on fire for God; they start serving God. Then all of a sudden, their spouse stops serving and starts trying to pull them away—and some people *will* walk away!

They think, "Well, I'm just trying to back up to catch my spouse and bring them up." I guarantee you that the moment you step back, you have proven to your spouse that you are not as godly a person as you said you were. That's why the Bible says that a husband can be converted by the conversation of his wife. That means that as a wife, you have to stay with what you know regardless of how he may act. *You* have to stay honorable, because when you hold to the code of honor, they will see it and begin to realize, "I am not going to change *you*, so *I* am going to have to change." But most people don't have the guts, the intestinal fortitude, whatever you want to call it, to stay and hold to the things of God! They'd much rather go home and sleep with their wife and not worry about what is honorable and what is not.

1 CORINTHIANS 11:23–32
For I have received of the Lord that which also I delivered unto you, that the Lord Jesus the same night in which he was betrayed took bread: And when he had given thanks, he brake it, and said, Take, eat: this is my body, which is broken for you: this do in remembrance of me. After the same manner also he took the cup, when he had supped, saying, this cup is the new testament in my blood: this do ye, as oft as ye drink it, in remembrance of me. For as often as ye eat this bread, and drink this cup, ye do shew the Lord's death till he come. Wherefore whosoever shall eat this bread, and drink

this cup of the Lord, unworthily, shall be guilty of the body and blood of the Lord. But let a man examine himself, and so let him eat of that bread, and drink of that cup. For he that eateth and drinketh unworthily, eateth and drinketh damnation to himself, not discerning the Lord's body. For this cause many are weak and sickly among you, and many sleep. For if we would judge ourselves, we should not be judged. But when we are judged, we are chastened of the Lord, that we should not be condemned with the world.

Many of you, if you've ever taken communion, have heard this. You should know this passage almost by heart by now. I want to bring something to your understanding—Paul was not there! On the night in question, on the night that he is speaking of, Paul was not present. So how did he get it? How does he know what happened? He tells you, he says the Lord told him! He says the Lord showed up and told him. We don't know exactly when that has happened, when he was caught up, but the Lord specifically showed him and told him these things that he's about to say. Many people don't put that together; they don't realize Paul was not there at the Last Supper. He wasn't present for that moment! But Jesus showed up personally and explained to him. So Paul says here, "That which I have received of the Lord, I am now sharing with you."

Let's break this down. Many people think this passage is only talking about communion. But while Paul is using communion as an example, he is talking about more than communion! If you read the context (chapters 10, 11, and 12) you will see that Paul is focusing on your working together with the Body—the part you play in the Body of Christ, your role as part of the Body as a whole, what you do in terms of how you affect the Body of Christ. So when he says that for this cause many are weak, sick, and some sleep or some die, he's not talking about taking communion or getting drunk off of communion wine! He's talking about not discerning what you are doing—in other words, indiscretion! He's talking about how you have to be discerning about what is going on as you take communion.

Often when a secular TV show has a representation of Catholicism, it will use this scripture to say that someone is not worthy of taking communion. That's not what these verses are saying! It's not saying that people are unworthy; it's saying the attitude and the manner in which you participate in communion need to discern the Lord's Body. So if Jesus is the head of the Body, then who is the Body? We are. If we are the Body, and He's the head, then to discern the Body would have to be how to discern all of us, and how to discern how each of us affects all of us.

So then, this is the reason why people are sick, weak, and die— that's why Paul said "for this cause."

Many people do not understand that for a believer's weakness to go to sickness and then to death, there has to be a cause. Now, I don't mean old age. I'm talking about stuff where you see things happen and you're like, "It doesn't even make any sense! How can somebody who's 26 be going through this? How can someone who's 30 be going through this?"

If you're a believer, you're either being tried or tested, or there's a cause. Something that is happening has caused this problem, and we have to be mindful of it. How are we affecting the Body? Because Paul said the moment someone gets to a place where they are affecting the Body in a bad way, "for this cause, many are weak, sick, and some die.".

Notice He said that if you judge yourself, then you won't be judged! He said that when we are judged, we're being corrected by God so that we won't be condemned with the world.

This is way deeper than a wafer and some grape juice!

What God wants us to understand from chapters 10, 11, and 12—and I guarantee that if you study it on your own, you will see exactly what the apostle Paul was trying to get the Corinthians to understand—is if you affect the Body in a negative way, then you cause disease in the Body.

I'll give you a very small example. Let's say people from the church are depending on you to do something for the church. You know what you're supposed to do, but you just decide you're not going to do it. Now other people have to scramble to cover you! You're causing a problem in the Body, and you're affecting other people!

You're sitting in the church while you're sleeping with somebody else's wife.

ROMANS 13:6–10
For for this cause pay ye tribute also: for they are God's ministers, attending continually upon this very thing. Render therefore to all their dues: tribute to whom tribute is due; custom to whom custom; fear to whom fear; honour to whom honour. Owe no man any thing, but to love one another: for he that loveth another hath fulfilled the law. For this, Thou salt not commit adultery, Thou shalt not kill, Thou shalt not steal, Thou shalt not bear false witness, Thou shalt not covet; and if there be any other commandment, it is briefly comprehended in this saying, namely, Thou shalt love thy neighbour as thyself. Love worketh no ill to his neighbour: therefore love is the fulfilling of the law.

How many times have you heard somebody say, "I don't owe no man anything but to love 'em"?

If you notice, people who say this use it as an excuse to say why they're not going to pay back something. Yet, in context, that is not what these verses mean! What is being said is "whatever you owe, pay it so that the only thing left that you owe someone is to love them."

If you keep going in Romans, it says all of the Ten Commandments are summed up in this one command. If all ten are equally important and equally different, then how can they all be summed up with one thing?

How can they be summed up with one statement: "Love your neighbor as you love yourself"?

Notice what these Commandments really are, and what God's saying to you! He's saying that when you steal from somebody, you've done harm to them. When you're sleeping with somebody's wife, somebody else's spouse, or whatever the case may be, you have done harm!

He said love worketh no harm to anyone else.

Here you see, even in the New Testament, that He's telling you that those who do things like that are operating in darkness!

ROMANS 13:12–14
The night is far spent, the day is at hand: let us therefore cast off the works of darkness, and let us put on the armour of light. Let us walk honestly, as in the day; not in rioting and drunkenness, not in chambering and wantonness, not in strife and envying. But put ye on the Lord Jesus Christ, and make not provision for the flesh, to fulfill the lusts thereof.

It's a lack of discernment that puts you in a place where you don't have the discretion to know you should not be doing certain things. It's darkness!

Stealing from people—you go through a drive-through, you give the cashier twenty bucks. You know your change is supposed to be two or three dollars, they give you thirteen dollars. You pull off and leave, thinking you just got the come-up.

"Well, they should learn how to count!" No, you should learn how to be honorable.

You should learn how not to steal.

Do you go to the store or a restaurant, or to a movie theater, and order water, then take that free cup and fill it with soda?

Love worketh no harm to anyone else. In everything you do, is anyone getting harmed in the process? Some person who's working a register at a restaurant ends up short ten dollars at the end of the day, and now their job is in jeopardy, but you got the come-up!

I don't know that everybody needs to hear this, but some people need to hear this. Because no one's teaching honor anymore! There's no code anymore of what's honorable and what isn't. There's no king in Israel, and everyone's doing what's right in their own eyes! And it's a sad place to be when people don't understand what is honorable. And I'm not going to cover up dishonor; I'm not going to accept dishonorable people, because when you associate with dishonor, that makes you dishonorable! Because regardless of what you say, if you want me to see who you are, all I have to do is look at your friends. The people you surround yourself with will always be an indication of who you are.

Giving honor is not sleeping with a married woman or a married man. Giving honor is not stealing from someone. Whatever is due to a person, give that. The apostle Paul runs down the list! Don't steal, don't covet, because those behaviors are dishonorable. And then he goes on to say that a person works no ill toward his neighbor, he devises no schemes against his neighbor—which is exactly what David did.

David came up with a scheme.

And as a result, David lost his first son with Bathsheba.

According to Old Testament law, if a man slept with another man's wife, both of them were supposed to be stoned to death. So Nathan came to David and said, "God spared you," because David was supposed to die!

One thing we have to realize now is that David's second son with Bathsheba was Solomon.

God is not unrighteous to forget your labor. David repented; he changed his heart; he made the adjustment—he married her, and then he had Solomon.

The issue was honor! God basically said, "You're the king! You're the one through whom I'm going to bring my son, and you're going to commit adultery and have a child out of it and think I'm going to let that slide? The price you'll have to pay is that this child you conceived through this situation is not going to make it."

Then David married Bathsheba, and the Bible says she conceived and had Solomon.

God cares about the order of things; He cares about the honor of things; He cares how you do stuff!

I've seen unmarried people say on Facebook how they're trying to have a baby, and post their little pregnancy tests, and I'm sitting there thinking, "Y'all don't think you've got the cart before the horse?"

God is all about honor! He's about how things are being handled. You walk around thinking, "Well, I love God and God loves me and that's all." No, you've got to stop watching that smiling preacher on TV who's telling you all these jokes and making you laugh, thinking everything's okay, because it's not!

Honor is important; honor will set the tone for what you walk in! Now, if you want to walk in average and mediocrity, then do what you do. But if you really want the fullness of what God has for you, you'd better understand honor!

This one indiscretion of David's set his whole family on edge—just one thing! David ended up fighting the backlash all the days of his life.

David's son Amnon slept with Tamar, and she turned to him and said, "It'd be one thing if you slept with me and then married me—just marry me. Make it right! But to have done this to me and then left me out there? To do such a thing is dishonorable."[27]

All David had to do was the right thing, and God would have blessed him, and Solomon could have been the first child! But David was not honorable, and he attacked an honorable man.

GENESIS 4:1–7
And Adam knew Eve his wife; and she conceived, and bare Cain, and said, I have gotten a man from the LORD. And she again bare his brother Abel. And Abel was a keeper of sheep, but Cain was a tiller of the ground. And in process of time it came to pass, that Cain brought of the fruit of the ground an offering unto the LORD. And Abel, he also brought of the firstlings of his flock and of the fat thereof. And the LORD had respect unto Abel and to his offering: But unto Cain and to his offering he had not respect. And Cain was very wroth, and his countenance fell. And the LORD said unto Cain, Why art thou wroth? and why is thy countenance fallen? If thou doest well, shalt thou not be accepted? and if thou doest not well, sin lieth at the door. And unto thee shall be his desire, and thou shalt rule over him.

---

27 This story is told in 2 Samuel 13.

Notice how it says Cain brought some of the fruit from the ground —in other words, he just grabbed some stuff, threw it in a bucket, brought it to God and said, "Hey, here you go."

Abel brought the fat from his first flocks. Let me help you with this. In an agrarian society, your first flocks are the ones that produce the next flocks. So if you have two, and your two can produce four, and four can produce eight, and eight can produce sixteen, there's a multiplication that comes. If I give you a piece of what's first, I slow down that table! Because if I have two and I give you one, now I have one! So now one goes to two, two goes to four, as opposed to two going to four and then to eight. So I have literally slowed down my progress by giving you the first parts of it.

Abel didn't care! Because he knew that God would make up the difference.

They both brought an offering, but God had honor for the one, and no honor for the other—and Cain knew it! And that's why Cain got all sour-faced, and God said, "What's your problem, man? Fix yo face! If you do right, won't I accept you too? If you honor Me, I'll honor you."

Honor wasn't about the amount. Honor wasn't even about the stuff. It was about the heart concerning it!

It's about how important dealing with things concerning God is to you, how significant it is to you, whether or not you even care. Let's say you're scheduled to serve, and you don't even care if you show up or don't show up; you don't care if you call or don't call; you don't care if your job gets in the way or doesn't get in the way. Besides, you've got to make a living!

And then people wonder, because if they think God doesn't care how they handle things, because they think, "God loves me no matter what I do, He loves me!"

Yes, God loves you, but we're talking about honor.

And He said, "If you honor Me, then I'll honor you."

Most people don't realize that the reason they don't see manifestations is because manifestations are God's way of honoring a person.

When you show up and your situation has changed for the better, and everybody's watching and wondering how that worked out for you? That's God honoring you!

When it didn't seem like it was going to work, and you were stuck between a rock and a hard place and everybody's watching and criticizing, and you come out and you don't even smell like smoke? That's God honoring you!

1 SAMUEL 2:30
Wherefore the LORD God of Israel saith, I said indeed that thy house, and the house of thy father, should walk before me for ever: but now the LORD saith, Be it far from me; for them that honour me I will honour, and they that despise me shall be lightly esteemed.

You know what it means to think lightly of something? It's to think it's no big deal!

I don't know if kids still say this, but there was a time when everything was "Whatever!" You'd address a problem and get "Whatever!"

You know what that was? It was thinking lightly of something that was important; to them it wasn't that important, so "Whatever!"

When your job gets more out of you than God does, you're saying, "Whatever!"

"I'm more committed to things than I am to God—whatever!"

"I'd rather be out on my boat than in church on Sunday—whatever!"

According to the New English Translation, God says "I will curse those who think lightly of Me."

You know how Proverbs 25:2 says that it's the glory of God to conceal a matter, but it's the honor of kings to search it out? People don't realize that when God reveals things to you, even how you treat your revelation can be dishonorable!

When you treat your revelation with dishonor—I've seen people be like, "Oh my God, I got it! It's revelation! It's straight from the throne! It makes my belly leap (or my baby leap in my belly)! Man, I've got it!" And two weeks later they've forgotten.

How you treat revelations God gives you is important! It's the glory or honor of God to conceal a matter, and the glory of kings to search it out. In other words, there's a benefit to you when you receive revelation and get understanding so that you can take the understanding (like Proverbs 5 just said) and apply it to knowledge, so you can discern what's right or wrong, so you can be led by the Holy Ghost in the midst of a situation and do what is honorable and right before the eyes of God.

But if you can't even hold on to revelation? If you don't treat it as precious or valuable or important or weighty? That's what honor means; honor means it's weighty to you! That the Word of God or the revelation that comes to you is so heavy, it's so important that there's nothing you would do to let it go, because you honor it!

So we have to ask ourselves, "Did God change His mind about Eli's family's priesthood?"

Because He said, "You were supposed to be My priests, but now be it far from Me."

So did God change His mind, or did they function in a way that was so dishonorable that they could not remain as priests? In other words, they shot their own selves. God was letting them know, "You have officially shot yourselves."

David repented; David changed! David said, "From this moment forward, I get it and I'm going to do this right, so I'm going to marry this woman! I'm going to be honorable concerning the situation."

And when he did it honorably, God said "Okay, now here comes Solomon, your heir."

The story had nothing to do with David's sexual indiscretions. It had everything to do with God's focus on honor; how you should deal with people in your life.

How do you deal with the honorable people God has placed in your life? How do you deal with your pastors, with your leaders?

How do you handle them? Do you handle them with disrespect, disregard, do you think lightly of them?

"It doesn't matter; who cares? I'll tell them anything I wanna tell them; I'll do whatever I'm going to do. I'll hurt the church; I'll steal from the church; I'll take from the church; I'll do whatever it takes; it doesn't matter to me." You've got to be a special kind of stupid!

I see people who are so critical and hurtful toward the church as a whole. I have to ask you: How do you think God—who set up the institution of the church, whose son Jesus said, "The gates of Hell shall not prevail against My church"—is going to feel about that?

How do you think that's going to turn out?

This is stuff I'm dealing with myself, personally! I am really working on myself to understand and to discern that everything God gives me, I have to treat as valuable. I have to treat them as weighty.

If God gave me a car, maybe it isn't the car I want right this precise second, but I need to be honorable about it. I need to treat it well; I need to make sure it stays washed; I need to make sure there aren't any french fries on the floor!

If God has given me a house, I take care of that house. I need to make sure that the house is clean from top to bottom.

I'm honorable toward the things I already have because I consider them weighty, I consider them significant, and I consider them important. And God is, in fact, watching!

He didn't care what the offering was; He cared about the heart behind how the offering was dealt with, how the things of God were approached.

He said to Abel, "You brought the firstlings; you brought the fat of the firstlings; you brought what was important! Your brother just scraped some stuff together!"

God cares how we handle things. God cares how we treat things.

It's like when God said in Exodus 23:29, "I'm gonna increase you, but I'm only going to do it slowly, lest the beasts of the field take over." Or in other words, "I can't give all this to you and you not handle it well, because if you can't take care of it, then the beasts of the field will come in and take it from you."

If you're complaining about mowing the lawn for one house, stop asking God for two. If you can't figure out how to hire a landscaper to take care of one house, don't delude yourself into thinking you're getting a second one.

It's only when you manage well what you already have, when you're honorable with what you already have, when you have the ability to have discretion and to understand how you're affecting other things around you—that's when you're being honorable.

When you treat God's gifts as light, as no big deal, whenever it's no big deal, you'll do whatever. If you think stealing from people is no big deal, you'll do it. You'll cover it up; you'll hide it; you'll allow it to happen; you'll watch it go down because you think it's just no big deal.

But if you think they're a serious offense, you will not tolerate certain things! You will not allow certain things in your life. And this is why God said, "What you honor, I will honor." It doesn't matter what it is. It matters whether or not you're honorable with it.

These are the things that separate those who are successful in God and those who struggle. This is really that place that separates them, because doesn't God love us all?

Of course He does.

1 SAMUEL 2:35
And I will raise me up a faithful priest, that shall do according to that which is in mine heart and in my mind: and I will build him a sure house; and he shall walk before mine anointed for ever.

After He makes it clear that they won't be involved anymore because of their dishonor, He says "I will raise Me up a faithful priest."

You can do something but not be doing it the way that's in His heart and mind.

"Well, I pray!" But do you do it the way that's in God's heart and in God's mind?

"I give when I can!" But do you do it in the way that's in God's heart and in God's mind?

Because if you won't do it the way God told you to do it?

People think it doesn't affect any other areas of their life, but a lot of things that people deal with are tied to their disobedience.

1 SAMUEL 2:36
And it shall come to pass, that every one that is left

**in thine house shall come and crouch to him for a
piece of silver and a morsel of bread, and shall say,
Put me, I pray thee, into one of the priests' offices,
that I may eat a piece of bread."**

They were supposed to be priests forever. It was Eli's lineage and
his family, and God said, "You're fired! Not only are you fired, but
everybody in your house will have nothing and you'll have to beg for
whatever it is that you want."

Their lack of honor didn't just affect their occupation; it didn't
even just affect them!

It affected everyone in their house; that doesn't seem fair!

Honor meant that much to God.

This is what I want you to understand. It isn't that God is trying to
hurt you, it's really the fact that when you operate in honor, you open
yourself up to so much more. And when you operate in dishonor, you
shut down God's ability to function because you're handling life in a
dishonorable way.

And then you want God to put His stamp on it.

And if you've made it this far being dishonorable, you'd better
bless God. But I can tell you this much—this is why people struggle.
This is why they don't see the power of God; this is why some people
stay sick. It's really because they're not honorable concerning the
things God has given them to do, asked them to do, assigned them to
do.

This is why when God tells me to go, I go.

This is why if God tells me to go help another church somewhere, I
go.

And I'll do it in a heartbeat.

A person who used to go to our church came to me and said, "Pastor, I need you to tell me whenever you're leaving so I know when not to come."

I'm thinking, "You're an idiot!"

First of all, if you're coming to see me, you've missed the point.

Stonepoint is a church, it's a body of believers, and God has a supply for that body whether I'm here or not. And to say that if I'm not here then you're not here—not only is that immature, but it's dishonorable toward the things that God is doing!

If I bring somebody into this church's pulpit to preach, that means I trust them. And you mean to tell me that I'm going to have people who won't show up to give this guest speaker honor because they think they don't have to render respect to whom respect is due, honor to whom honor is due?

I am going to go do exactly what God has told me to do when He tells me to do it and how He tells me to do it—because if He took the time to tell me, it's precious and it's weighty to me; it's important to me. And if He gave me something, whatever He gave me is important to me, it's weighty to me, and I'm not going to run around coveting what I do not have.

I'm going to honor what I do have, and watch God increase me, watch God give me favor, watch God move in my life when other people are paying twice what I'm paying.

And it will be because God has moved, not because I've obtained it in dishonorable ways.

CHAPTER 7

INCREDULOUS

Let's look at 2 Kings 7:1–2:

> **Then Elisha said, Hear ye the word of the LORD; Thus saith the LORD, To morrow about this time shall a measure of fine flour be sold for a shekel, and two measures of barley for a shekel, in the gate of Samaria. Then a lord on whose hand the king leaned answered the man of God, and said, Behold, if the LORD would make windows in heaven, might this thing be? And he said, Behold, thou shalt see it with thine eyes, but shalt not eat thereof.**

It's interesting that this verse tells us that the man of God said some things—and this particular individual recognized that it was, in fact, a man of God speaking—and the man of God was speaking what the Lord had said. As he was speaking what the Lord had said, he was revealing to them, in other words, that by that same time the next day, they would be able to buy a five-pound bag of flour for a nickel.

They were in a drought. They were in a recession, and here he's saying, "Things are about to change, and I'm letting you know."

And this dude's like, "Well, I know God can open up the heavens, but

Elisha says, "Well, you'll see it! But since you're questioning it, you won't partake in it."

Or in other words, "Since you've got a problem and won't believe in what God has told you, you'll see it—but you won't eat none of it!"

1 TIMOTHY 1:12–13
And I thank Christ Jesus our Lord, who hath enabled me, for that he counted me faithful, putting me into the ministry; Who was before a blasphemer, and a persecutor, and injurious: but I obtained mercy, because I did it ignorantly in unbelief.

People don't necessarily understand how when we're told things, when things are shared with us from the pulpit, utterance is greatly dependent upon the hearer.

As a pastor, my responsibility is to teach it. Your responsibility is to hear it and receive it.

An old Midwest colloquialism says something like this: "Sometimes you've got to tell people how the cow eats the cabbage." In other words, sometimes you've gotta tell people as straight as it is, as real as it is, and you can't be going around in circles about it.

So our next word is INCREDULOUS.

When a person is incredulous, it means they have information, but won't believe it.

In other words, you done been told—but you're choosing not to believe it!

Many people think that all unbelief is the same.

Unbelief is not all the same. You can have an unbelief that is based on the fact that you've never been told, and that's ignorance. Ignorance can be rectified by hearing the truth. (Or in other words, getting told how the cow eats the cabbage!)

In verse 13, Paul is talking about himself, but he's telling us, basically, "The reason I obtained mercy is because I did this out of ignorance. I didn't know any better. I was attacking the church, persecuting the church, blaspheming. I was living as a chief sinner, but not because I knew better and wouldn't do better."

One of my challenges is that it's very frustrating to teach messages that are designed to bless and help people and then watch them backslide and reject what they've heard.

A pastor's greatest desire—a true pastor's, that is—is wanting to see people grow.

I want to see people develop; I want to see people walk in the fullness of all God has for them. So when I begin to see different things—the stupidity people can put themselves into—I feel frustrated. I really want people to grow. And because I want them to grow, I end up teaching messages that are a little hard. But I'm telling you, your response is what changes the outcome—because utterance is greatly affected by the hearer.

> **Hebrews 3:12, 19**
> **Take heed, brethren, lest there be in any of you an evil heart of unbelief, in departing from the living God. ... So we see that they could not enter in because of unbelief.**

So we see here that we are not able to enter because of unbelief.

Unbelief has a lot of different meanings or can come from different places.

In this context, unbelief is that they heard it—they just didn't want to respond to what they heard!

In other words, it's been preached. They've heard it over and over again and yet they are stiff-necked, or they have become hardhearted, and now they cannot seem to hear what is being told to them.

So we have to recognize that just because someone operates in unbelief doesn't mean they're ignorant. A lot of people who operate in unbelief have heard the Word—they were just incredulous. And that is completely dishonorable to God, because once you've heard it—you know the scripture?

We're responsible for it!

This is why coming up the light is so significant. Think about Uzzah, who was following the Ark when David was returning it to Jerusalem. He reached up and touched the Ark because he thought it was going to fall off the oxcart—and God struck him dead because he touched the Ark of the Covenant.

Now, the same Ark was with the Philistines, and the Philistines were trying to figure out why all these calamities were befalling their lives—and it's because they had taken God's presence.

So here they've taken the Ark, and they've decided "Here's what we're gonna do. We're gonna take the Ark; we're going to put it on a cart; we're gonna attach some milk cows to it that just had babies, and if the milk cows return to their children, that's what their natural inclination is to do. That's what they know to do; that's naturally what they're supposed to do. But if those milk cows take off and take that cart back to Israel, we know that the only way that's possible is God had to make that happen."

So they put this thing on a cart, and the milk cows took it and left. They did not go back to their calves.

Now, the point I'm getting at is nobody here was struck dead for mishandling the Ark— so why would Uzzah get struck dead?

Because he knew better.

See, a lot of times people don't understand that you're accountable whether you want to be or not.

JEREMIAH 18:12
And they said, There is no hope: but we will walk after our own devices, and we will every one do the imagination of his evil heart.

You know, you have a decision to make every time you hear the truth. The Bible says the Word is the truth, and it's bizarre to me how many people live in a place where they can listen to the Word and then literally walk away and do exactly what was in their heart and not what they heard the Word say. They will follow the stubbornness of the evil nature of their heart faster than they'll follow the ordinances of God. I'm not implying that anyone is perfect—what I'm trying to help you understand is that there's a difference between being ignorant and being incredulous. There's a difference between "I don't know any better" and "I'm choosing not to function in faith" or "I'm choosing to operate in a place of unbelief."

See, when you're incredulous, it means you think that what you just heard is so farfetched that it's absolutely impossible to believe it.

It's like if I told you that I jumped off the top of this building, landed on the ground, did two somersaults, and then jumped back up on top of the building and took the elevator down.

You'd be like, "Pastor, that sounds a little impossible!"

149

Well, it is, and it didn't happen—but the Word of God is real, and the Bible says the Word of God is truth.

The difference between being ignorant and being incredulous is a hardening of your heart.

Have you ever had a callus on your hand?

If you've had a callus, you know that in the spot where the callus is, your feeling and sensitivity are off? It doesn't feel the same.

You lose sensitivity; you lose the ability to feel what's happening.

So it's interesting that the Bible tells us to guard our hearts with all diligence. When you guard your heart with all diligence, you will protect your heart from becoming too callous—because if your heart becomes callous, you don't know what's right or wrong anymore.

You don't have the ability to discern what's good or bad anymore.

We instruct people who work in our congregational care ministry that you can't trust what everybody says as to why they leave our church, because the truth is that most people lie about why they leave a church. They're not going to tell you the truth, because the truth is usually that what is being taught or what is being demanded of them is beyond what they are willing to do, because they're incredulous.

There's something in them that knows "I can't keep living this way. But every time I go there, I'm getting hit on the head with something that I don't want to deal with. I'm getting hardened over it, so now the only option I see is to pull myself out of it so I can get some peace." The peace that Satan brings; not the peace that God brings!

Then all of a sudden they're like, "Oh my gosh, see? I knew I'd feel better!" No, you yielded to what Satan wanted. And because you did what Satan wanted, you are now no longer a threat.

2 CORINTHIANS 6:11
O ye Corinthians, our mouth is open unto you, our heart is enlarged.

Paul is saying here, "When I speak to you, I'm open to you. I'm open so that you can be open. When I deal with you, I am so open with my heart—I'm not withholding anything from you. I don't withhold affection from you, and you haven't withheld yours from me. We have such openness between us that I can speak to you as children, because your heart is open."

The first thing people do when their hearts become callous is they start shutting down.

They're no longer open to their pastor. They're no longer open to the church. They're no longer open to other people. They start shutting down, hiding and disappearing.

If you can't bring yourself to have discussions and to be open and vulnerable about what's going on inside you, you've hardened your heart.

If you can't be open, that's a problem! In openness, things begin to be exposed, and you have the opportunity to get things right.

But when you avoid conversations about certain subjects, when you are ticked off, when you're sitting there like "Why does Pastor keep talking about this," it's because you don't get it.

Because if you got it, you would act differently.

The flow of the Holy Ghost brings correction to things that need to be dealt with, so that you can continue to go better, deeper, and further in the things of God.

If it always hits a sensitive spot for you, that's a sign that your heart's getting hardened! You're not wide open anymore. You're getting shut down … and shut down … and shut down, and you don't want to hear it. You don't want to talk about it. You don't want anybody else getting in. It's a complete lockdown of anyone trying to get close.

EXODUS 7:22
And the magicians of Egypt did so with their enchantments: and Pharaoh's heart was hardened, neither did he hearken unto them; as the LORD had said.

One of the strongest attributes of your heart being hardened is when you begin to side with people who are siding with your predilection, and not your promise.

You begin to listen to people who are reaffirming stupidity.

You'd rather listen to your drinking buddies than to your pastor.

You'd rather hang with your drug buddies than listen to what your church is saying.

Your wife is trying to talk to you, or your husband is trying to talk to you, and you listen to your guy friends or your girlfriends instead.

You're siding with people who are siding with your predilection, which is what you desire or what you want. The efforts of your flesh, the hardness of your heart—you're siding with that over your promise!

That's why our verse says the pharaoh wouldn't even listen to Moses and Aaron!

His heart was hardened—why?

Because the people by his side were feeding his ear garbage and he believed it!

"We can do it too; we can do this too! There is another way to do this. You don't have to do it that way! It's not so serious. It's not that big a deal. It's not a problem. Come on out to the club with us. Come on out and do this with us. There's no big deal here. It doesn't matter how you handle things. God could care less about how you handle stuff."

Remember how God reversed the curse on Israel and honored David with a second son by Bathsheba after he repented and acted honorably toward her and toward God. And that second son was Solomon.

People have no idea, the honor that is required. Now listen, I'll be honest with you—Can you live a life without honor toward God?

You sure can.

Can you skate through it and maybe nothing will happen?

Probably, it's possible.

But the people *I'm* talking to are the ones who can't handle average—they can't handle mediocrity; they want better!

I am not trying to tell you that you won't make it to heaven. I'm not trying to tell you that huge calamity will follow you in your life. What I'm trying to tell you is that if you really want the fullness of all that God has for you—if you're tired of low-level thinking, running around with low-level people and getting low-level outcomes—then you should understand this. If you learn how to increase your level of honor toward the things of God and toward God himself, He will increase the honor He bestows upon you! And then you'll be wondering, "How in the *world* did I miss it for so long?"

It's amazing how people can ignore the wisdom that would better their lives.

They just ignore it! They'll come to church, go through the motions, and just ignore it.

They're like, "Oh, that wasn't for me. That's for somebody behind me." No, it's for you!

The fact that you decided to shovel it onto somebody else should tell you that.

MATTHEW 24:12
And because iniquity shall abound, the love of many shall wax cold.

Notice what that's saying: The more sin abounds, the harder it is for people to love.

I've seen people disconnect from everything. They'll stop talking to people they used to talk to. They'll stop responding to phone calls. They'll stop connecting with people. They'll stop hanging out with people. They'll completely withdraw from people they professed to love just yesterday!

"Pastor, I love you, Pastor! I love you so much!"

Every time I hear people say "I love you," I'm like, "We'll see."

You go through memories and pictures, and you see people who *swore* they loved you. Yet their love waxed cold. And it's usually because of their sin, because of things in their life that I have nothing to do with. I didn't force them into that life.

I'm not the one they're drinking with.

I'm not the one they're having sex with.

I'm not the one they're partying with.

I have nothing to do with those choices, but once a person gets into those types of situations, their love waxes cold. Because wherever iniquity abounds, love can't. And in that place, nothing is more important than themselves. That's how a heart gets hardened. And once the heart gets hardened?

Boy, it's a tough place to be.

1 JOHN 1:5–9
This then is the message which we have heard of him, and declare unto you, that God is light, and in him is no darkness at all. If we say that we have fellowship with him, and walk in darkness, we lie, and do not the truth: But if we walk in the light, as he is in the light, we have fellowship one with another, and the blood of Jesus Christ his Son cleanseth us from all sin. If we say that we have no sin, we deceive ourselves, and the truth is not in us. If we confess our sins, he is faithful and just to forgive us our sins, and to cleanse us from all unrighteousness.

Notice that he says we lie when we *do* not the truth—not we lie when we *speak* not the truth, but when we *do* not the truth. Because you can't just *say* you are a Christian.

You can't just *say* you are a believer. You cannot *say* you're walking in light and not actually walk in it, because be not deceived— 1 John goes on to say that we are righteous as He is righteous.

Dealing with our soul—our mind, will, and emotions—is a process of growth and development. Although positionally and spiritually we are the righteousness of God in Christ, throughout this life on earth, we have to contend with our flesh and our soul. So we are never going to be able to walk in the same level of righteousness as Christ himself. But that should not stop us from aspiring to become better than who we used to be as God develops us into a perfect/mature man or woman.

When you become complacent and love your fleshly self enough to say, "I'm just okay with being just okay," then there's the problem right there. You should always have a constant desire to improve, to evolve and become better and say, "I'm going to be more and more like Christ. I'm going to allow God to change me, and to mold me, and to shape me, and to bring me into the next place He has for me, because I have been here for too long. I've been circling this mountain far too long."

There are so many people wondering, "Why am I not advancing? Why am I not moving forward? Why do things seem to be stagnant?" Because you keep circling the same mountain over and over again, and you refuse to deal with what your heart has become hardened to.

And because you won't deal with it, you're going to keep going around and around and around until the moment comes where you finally say, "I surrender my all! I don't care if I like it; I don't care if I agree with it—if it's the Word of God, then I'll submit to it and I'll watch God move in my life in such a way that all the people who said I was nothing will see me rise as they're on their way down, because I'll make the adjustments!"

Have you ever wondered why some people seem like as soon as they can't get something together, they start moving off, and off, and off, and off, and off?

They can't recover from a snare. It's almost like the moment they start entertaining something stupid, it starts working them. And next thing you know, they're getting further and further away from freedom in the truth. They don't even see it.

I'm going, "Do you know how *off* you really are?"

They don't, because God doesn't say, "In *darkness* is light." He says, "In *light* is light."

See, if you won't walk in the light of the words you have, you don't qualify for more light. And the only way you're going to *get* more light is to correct what you have gotten off into, get back over into the light, and allow God to reveal more. So many people get into darkness and think they're operating in light—this is why the Bible says that Satan can come disguised!

Proverbs 4:18-19 says that we increase in light as the day goes by. Day by day we get brighter and brighter, and that's the same type of light; that's God's light.

The light Satan brings is not God's light. That's why the Bible says to be careful of those who confuse light and darkness—because if your eye is dark, you'll do dark stuff and think it's light. You'll superimpose a godly perspective on something you know is wrong.

That's why the Apostle John said that in darkness, *there is no light.* And you are not going to be getting all of these revelations when you're sitting at home, twiddling your thumbs, being stubborn and insubordinate and incredulous towards God.

Some of the people who are the most disobedient are the ones you see all over Facebook giving spiritual advice to everybody else. They don't go to church, and they talk about being rebellious!

Like, *seriously*?

It is amazing to me how darkness will begin to work in the children of light.

God is everywhere.

I'm not talking about the presence of God here; I'm talking about light—I mean the Presence of God can be present, but light does not show up.

Light is revelation. Light is clarity. Light is understanding. Light is what's being revealed to you. Light is discerning the plans, purposes, and pursuits of God. The light is when you know the calling that's on your life and you are careful about how you handle things. You don't just get yourself hooked up in all kinds of relationships with people who are not like-driven, because the next thing that'll happen is they'll pull you right out of your church! And then you're siding with people who are speaking to your predilection, not your promise.

They know exactly what to say to you to sour your supply.

They know exactly what to say to you to mess you up.

"I can't believe the pastor does stuff like that. He uses generic toilet paper instead of Charmin!" And because they know that's a predilection issue of yours, all of a sudden that personal preference becomes a big deal when the truth of the matter is that the job of a pastor is to *feed you.*

I can tell you with all confidence, if you can sit in church when the Word is preached and not get fed, you ain't hungry! That's the truth.

God loves giving us revelation. God gives us so much, and I am very grateful for it.

But are you?

Or are you only grateful for what God gives you when it lines up with what you think—when it lines up with your predilection?

1 John says when we have light, we have fellowship one with another.

The first thing that tells you a person's hardened their heart is they break fellowship.

All of a sudden you're wondering, "Hey, where's So-and-so? What happened to So-and-so?"

When they first come into the church, they sit in the back. And then after they've worked their way up, they sit in the front row. They're receiving, they're getting it, and then all of a sudden they've worked their way back until the next thing you know, they're so far back that they're outside.

Paul said "I did these things, and there was mercy for me because I did them out of ignorance. But once I heard the truth, once the gospel got hold of me—"

Paul didn't say, "All right, listen y'all—I used to kill thousands, and I've only killed one today! The Lord is working on me!"

"I used to drink like a fish. I only had one drink today! The Lord is working on me!"

When Paul had an encounter with the Lord, everything changed in that divine moment!

People say things like, "I'm waiting for God to work something out of me. I'm waiting for God to burn this out of me. I'm waiting for God to change my heart." No, there's a point where if you are serious about the things of God and you heard the Word, you've got to move by faith.

Paul tells Timothy he's not even worthy, but what qualified him was his belief. And he struggled with unbelief, but it was because he was ignorant. When the truth came to him, he made adjustments. When the truth was revealed, he came to the place of saying, "You know what? It's time to change." And he did it!

Faith means moving in what you know the Word of God says, despite how you feel about it.

Too many people have gotten to the place where all they want to talk about is what they feel.

"Well, I feel like this, and I feel like that!" Listen, none of that matters.

I've been in situations where I have taught certain things *specifically* for certain people to get it right, but their heart was so hardened—and it's not that they were ignorant!

Other people see their situation and feel sorry for them—"Oh, poor baby!" No!

They have hardened their hearts. There's nothing you can do for a person who has hardened their heart. I'm gonna tell you how the cow ate the cabbage! It's the truth.

This is why when you get light, you walk in it. This is why we don't cast pearls before swine; because if you value the light you have, you don't give it to everybody, because not everybody is ready to hear it.

> **EPHESIANS 4:17–19**
> **This I say therefore, and testify in the Lord, that ye henceforth walk not as other Gentiles walk, in the vanity of their mind, Having the understanding darkened, being alienated from the life of God through the ignorance that is in them, because of the blindness of their heart: Who being past feeling have given themselves over unto lasciviousness, to work all uncleanness with greediness.**

One of the biggest challenges people have is not being attentive to warning signs.

Like, if your car starts to vibrate when you hit 60 or 70 miles per hour. If you put your hand on the steering wheel, and the steering wheel is shaking, then you know it's the front end. There's an alignment issue in the front, a tire issue, *something* in the front of the car. If your butt's shaking, if it's literally the seat that's shaking, you know that it's the back of the car and something's going on in the rear. That's a warning sign; you need to pay attention.

Now, here's what I've learned:

My first car was a Ford Escort—two-door, '87 or '85.

My next car was a Geo Metro, and I've progressed through different cars over the years.

One thing I've learned about cars is that if you sense *anything* is wrong? You'd better deal with it quickly!

Because if you ignore the signs, what starts out as a $200–$300 repair, could be *thousands*. One air strut for my car is $2,400!

So when you notice something, when a light comes on, you pay attention! Right?

When your heart lacks sensitivity, it's like calluses on your hands. You don't feel things like you normally should feel. You don't discern the warning signs when you start losing interest in things that you used to be passionate about.

One day it's "I love my church," and the next day, we can't find you.

Ephesians 4:17 is like a couple being together and everybody around them wondering, "What is she doing with him? What's he doing with her?" Under normal circumstances, she would know he's not right for her.

Their sensitivity to a sermon about things that should be done and not be done, how to handle things properly and how not to handle things—it's gone. The sensitivity is gone! Now they live life for lustful pleasure, and now they're eager to practice any kind of impurity.

Before, they chose to not go to the club anymore; now they're like, "Yeah, I'll go! What's wrong with a little bit of this? What's wrong with a little bit of that? Oh, you people are just too serious! You guys are religious!" No, we're righteous.

We're not perfect. We all have issues we struggle with, but we're not out there just doing whatever, not eagerly chasing after things we know are just completely wrong.

They have no sense of shame. They live for lustful pleasure, eagerly practicing every kind of impurity. They're swift to run to it—and the further away they get, the easier it is to entice them into things they should not be mixed up in. And the Bible says they are ever going after more.

It's the next drunken stupor; it's the next party; it's the next high; it's the next girl, the next woman, the next man. It's constant. They're thinking like worldly people; they're confused in how they think—and because of that, their understanding becomes darkened.

Once you get off into the darkness, you don't get any light.

I literally have seen people smoking, high on weed, talking about how they got a revelation.

"God speaks to me when I'm high." No, *a god* speaks to you.

There's no question, *a god* does speak to you!

Listen, if you look up the word "witchcraft" in the New Testament? The word for "witchcraft" is *pharmakeia.* like "pharmacy." Drugs put you into an altered state in which you begin to have an alternate reality, in which you live in an alternate place doing alternate things.

"I feel closest to God when I'm high." No you don't!

This is what happens when you get into the futility of your own thinking.

This is what happens when you side with your proclivities, and not your promise.

162

This is what happens when you play with things or with people who take you out of the will of God. While they were dating you, they came to your church. Then, suddenly, once you've gotten hooked, that's when they stop.

"Now we don't have to do all of that, because now I got you."

I've seen it over and over and over and over again, and it's usually because they've walked into darkness. Boy meets girl, boy likes girl; he's growing, trying to do church. Girl has sex with boy, boy thinks nobody knows. Now she's gotten him off into darkness, and it's just a matter of time.

"Well, Pastor, can't you preach to them?"

No.

"Why?"

Because their heart's hardened.

Now, if they were to correct the situation, if he would tell her, "You know what? We're gonna do this the right way, so no more of this funny business until we've had conversations about getting married and being honorable, because I believe the Word, and the Word says what it says," that would be a different story. And if she leaves? Buh-bye!

But see, so many people struggle with that.

"Well, I just don't know what I'd do by myself." I know what you'd do. You'd do the same thing you're doing now. Trust God.

It's hard dealing with an incredulous person, because you have to ask yourself if they were ignorant.

You can fix ignorance! You can't fix stupid.

So many people are trying to fix stupid and are getting frustrated. So many people are trying to find a way to correct a hardened heart and they tell themselves, "I'm just going to love them into a better heart." How is that possible? They're not open!

The Bible says a pastor goes after a sheep. He leaves the 99 sheep, and goes after a *sheep*. Not wolves, not goats—*sheep*. How do you know a sheep? Its heart isn't hardened.

They just have gotten into a bad place because they're ignorant.

That's why Paul said, "I did this ignorantly. I didn't know. There's mercy for me because I didn't know any better."

So here comes Paul, riding on his horse. God knocks him off his horse.

First thing he says is, "Is that you, Lord?"

He didn't say "Which one of y'all kicked me!"

Think about that.

He literally got knocked off his high horse, and the first thing he said was "Is that you, Lord?"

He knew revelation had just hit, and God said, "Okay, now listen, you've been running around here acting ignorant long enough. Now I have a purpose for your life, and because I have a purpose for your life, let Me help you at this point. You're not stupid, you just didn't know any better. So why are you attacking My people? Why are you kicking against the pricks? Why are you doing these things?"

And he said, "I just didn't know. So help me."

And the Lord began to deal with him and to show him things. Paul ended up writing two-thirds of the New Testament.

He said, "Of the sinners, I'm chief. I'm trying to help you to see something. I'm the worst of the worst, but when I get it, I've got it."

You want to know how to gauge people? Do they hear it and make the adjustment, or do they side with their predilection and literally walk out of their promise? Is their proclivity so strong, is the thing they desire the most so strong, that it takes them right out of the will, the purpose, and the plan that God has for their life? You have to ask yourself, if a person can't be loyal to God, how are they ever going to be loyal to you? How are they going to be loyal?

Typically when people do things that violate their morals, their internal code, it's called lack of congruence. It's the idea that whatever I do has to line up with what I really believe and if I start doing things that don't really line up well at some point in time, I have to disconnect from it because it's a constant pulling and knowing and nagging, and it begins to create irritation.

Years ago, we had a lady in our church who was a very big giver. One day, I got to talking about alcohol in my sermon. I honestly had no idea she struggled with alcohol. She got so mad she left the church. I remember thinking, "Now what are we going to do?"

At our next service, more new people came, and we never felt the issue of her loss.

Now, her leaving wasn't because she was offended by something I had done to her. She was offended by the Word. Listen to me, I am here to offend your mind, to reveal your heart and its indicator.

Your car's blinker is designed to show which way you plan to go so that other drivers have an indication of what you're about to do, right?

The indicator on your heart telegraphs when your heart becomes hardened. You can't even see the blinkers anymore. You don't even know what the instrument panel is telling you. You become so disconnected that all you have is anger, frustration, boiling, percolating. All the while, the blinker's going off; the instrument panel is telling you, "Don't do this, don't go down this road! This is a bad place to be!"

The Holy Ghost inside you is saying, "Don't do that!"

And then you pray, "God, if you don't want me to be with this man, take him away." The dumbest stuff I've ever heard in my life. He didn't bring that guy to you in the first place.

That's like buying something at Macy's then walking into JC Penney and saying, "I bought this at Macy's, but I want to return it to you."

They didn't sell it to you! Don't allow these things to come into your life, because this is what causes you to harden your heart and become incredulous.

God cares about how you honor Him.

I've got to wrestle with some people about giving their time. It's not that they don't know better—they know better! But their heart has hardened on the issue. There's nothing else to talk about anymore.

You've got to protect yourself against allowing your heart to be hardened in certain places. You have to get back into the light. You don't have the luxury of allowing your heart to get hardened in areas you don't want to talk about.

If this message nails your hide to the wall, you need to grab your hide and say, "Thank you, God, for nailing my hide. I sure do appreciate it. This is precious and valuable. This is a place where I need to make an adjustment, and I'm going to go ahead and make that adjustment."

Get out of the darkness, get back into the light. We're going to go on with God and do all that God has called us to do, because we're not going to stay in a place where we should not be. I don't know about you, but I don't want to have to go through all that kind of stuff—especially when I don't have to, especially when God is merciful, and *especially* when God says that all I've got to do is quit being stupid!

CHAPTER 8

INFIDELITY

Take a look at 1 Samuel 2:30:

> **Wherefore the LORD God of Israel saith, I said indeed that thy house, and the house of thy father, should walk before me for ever: but now the LORD saith, Be it far from me; for them that honour me I will honour, and they that despise me shall be lightly esteemed.**

People often hear me thanking God for a revelation, thanking God for giving me further instructions. Or I'll thank the Holy Ghost for bringing something to remembrance—publicly, out loud! The reason I do that is because I count everything God gives me as weighty. It's important to me, and I want Him to know it immediately, and I want others to know it, too! When you honor things, you treat them as important, and you treat them as significant. There are times when God will reveal things to you; He'll teach you something by revelation or by the anointing, and if you're not careful, you'll just dismiss it! You'll act like it's not important, like it's not significant or weighty.

The older I get, the more I realize what I don't know and what other people *really* don't know. I think the younger people are, the more they seem to think or assume that everybody knows everything. As they gain a little more experience, they begin to realize that other people don't know anything—and neither do they!

So it's so important that, when you have revelation or when God reveals things to you, you are grateful for it—that you are honorable about it, that you thank God for it, and that you then walk in it. Because if He revealed it to you, He revealed it to you for a reason!

Years ago, God talked to a friend of mine about watching television. Another friend from the same church decided to move in with that friend, and I said to him, "You do realize that God talked to him about not having a television, right?"

And he said, "Yeah, I know, but what does that have to do with me?"

I said, "You're moving into his house."

He said, "Well, I'm sure he'll let me have a television!"

I said, "I don't think so. You might want to talk to him about it!"

So they got to talking about it, and sure enough, I was right—he wasn't allowed to bring a television. So he was watching stuff on his phone, trying to figure out how to have some level of entertainment in his life. The longer this went on, the more upset he became, and finally he came to me and said, "I think I'm gonna approach him and talk to him about this TV thing."

I said, "Why?"

He said, "Well, don't you think that's legalistic?"

I said, "Hold on! Let me see if I understand this correctly. God told him to do something, and you are wondering if I have an opinion—on what *God Almighty* told him to do?"

"Well, I just think it's legalistic."

I said, "Well, I just think you should move!"

When God begins to talk to you about doing things, or about how to handle a situation, or how to work a certain thing, you might be very disrespectful about how you handle that. You can disregard it, ignore it —that's why we talked about being incredulous in the last chapter.

With incredulous people, it's not that they don't know better! They know better, they just won't do better. You've got to be careful, because they'll tug on your heartstrings and you'll start feeling sorry for them! You'll be wondering how you or the church can help them, but you can't help someone whose heart is hardened to the truth. You can't help people whom you love more than they love themselves, and you can't help anybody who loves himself or herself more than God.

This is why we pastors are told to go after sheep—not wolves, not goats; *sheep.*

Sheep follow. When you call a sheep, it knows your voice.

Let me help you understand something; sheep have very poor eyesight. If you didn't know that, now you know! They have *very* poor eyesight, and that's why they know their shepherd's voice. When they hear the voice of the shepherd, they can follow the voice and return to where they belong.

When you don't know your shepherd's voice, what are you going to do?

You're going to get lost.

This is why so many people struggle in their lives—because they can't hear counsel, because they don't know their shepherd's voice. They're too used to listening to all the other voices in their head!

I take church very seriously.

You wanna know why? *Because God instituted it.*

I take giving very seriously. I take *everything* concerning God, and concerning the things God has revealed to me, very seriously. The Bible says we are accountable for the things that are revealed to us!

Whatever you don't know, you will not be held accountable for. Whatever is a secret thing to God, that belongs to Him. But whatever has been revealed to you—you are responsible to walk in it!

To lightly esteem these things, to think nothing of them, to think they're no big deal—if you think anything concerning God is no big deal, that's a problem! When you want God to honor you, you'd better honor Him because that's what qualifies you to walk in all the things God has for you.

1 SAMUEL 2:35
And I will raise me up a faithful priest, that shall do according to that which is in mine heart and in my mind: and I will build him a sure house; and he shall walk before mine anointed for ever.

Remember what He said a faithful priest is? One who does things the way they are in God's heart and in God's mind. He called that faithful.

So many people struggle with the idea of what "faithful" really is. They think "faithful" just means that they show up—that's not "faithful"! "Faithful" means you are diligent, and that you are really after the things of God, that you are focused on doing things the way the God said to do them.

I think it's tragic how many times people get into relationships outside of wedlock, and things happen, tragedies happen, and I wonder, "Was it worth it?" Was it worth it to create so many problems and so much stress not doing things God's way? Now, tragedies do happen, and so many horrible things can occur, but these situations occurred because people were not doing things the way God said to do them.

If people took time to get to know the person they're going to marry and have babies with, and they spent time understanding that person and really getting to know that person, a lot of marriages would last better—because people would have actually spent time learning who they're about to jump into bed with. When they don't take the time to prepare for marriage, then they'll get counseled through the enemy they're sleeping with, when they should have just entered into the relationship the correct way to begin with. There's a way things are supposed to be done, y'all!

It was significant and important to me that before I married my wife, I had her in front of my spiritual father. I had her in front of my spiritual father's spiritual father. I needed everybody—people I trust, people who are around me, people who are responsible for my spiritual wellbeing—to be around her and to get an assessment of her before I married her. You wanna know why? Because it's important. It's *the rest of my life!* She had to pass a few tests!

Things are supposed to work a certain way. When you're honorable toward God and how you handle life, God begins to honor you—because you were honorable in the way you handled what He brought you. This is why the Bible says that if there's anything you owe to Caesar, pay Caesar. Anybody you owe honor to, honor them. Anybody you owe respect to, respect them. Whatever it is that you're supposed to do, do it—because people are watching you!

People are observing what you do, and the way you handle things. The ends do not justify the means. I don't care what anybody says, *the ends do not justify the means.*

People will say "Well, as long as we got the end result...." No, that's not it!

How you handled it is important to God. That's why God says, "Don't be unequally yoked."

How do you know if you're unequally yoked?

If you fight over stuff that you shouldn't have to fight over when it comes to the things of God, you're unequally yoked. It's that simple.

1 TIMOTHY 1:12–13
And I thank Christ Jesus our Lord, who hath enabled me, for that he counted me faithful, putting me into the ministry; Who was before a blasphemer, and a persecutor, and injurious: but I obtained mercy, because I did it ignorantly in unbelief.

In the last chapter, we discussed two types of unbelief. There's the unbelief that results from ignorance ("I don't know any better so I can't do better, thus I do what I know") and then there's unbelief that results from being incredulous.

Paul said, "The reason why I was so injurious and blasphemous, the reason why I did the things that I did is because I was ignorant. It wasn't that I knew better and didn't do better; I just didn't know."

Not all unbelief is the same thing, within the same category. Some people have hardened hearts! They've got it in their heads that "this is the way I'm gonna do it, and I don't care what anybody thinks about it; I'm just gonna do this my way and it is what it is." And that's why they keep falling on their behinds—because that's pride. And pride always comes before a fall.

Paul said, "He counted me faithful, and so He enabled me." So the "I" of this chapter is INFIDELITY.

The technical definition of "infidelity" is not "being unfaithful in a relationship of a sexual nature."

When a husband and wife are having marital problems, one of the first questions a counselor asks is "Was there any infidelity?" So our society associates the word "infidelity" with *sexual* unfaithfulness. However, I want you to back up on the broader sense of infidelity as "not being faithful to what you're supposed to be faithful to." That's the bigger, overarching definition of infidelity. It's not being faithful.

Infidelity was the issue when God said, "Who honors Me, I will honor." He was saying, in other words, "If you're honorable toward Me, you'll be faithful not only to Me, but also to the way that I want things done." Paul said, "The reason why God put me in ministry is because He counted me faithful."

Let me tell you something: many are called—*many* are called—but few are chosen. One of the greatest reasons Christians get so frustrated is because they know there's a call of God on their life, they understand there's something God wants them to do, but they start getting impatient with it because they expect more than what they themselves give. In other words, if you are asked to do something and you are told, "This is what I need you to do," your ability to be faithful to do that thing demonstrates your ability to be promoted to do something else.

Paul said, basically, "The reason why God enabled me, why God graced me, why God gave me a supernatural ability to accomplish the task, is because He counted me faithful."

So many people want the grace and the enablement to do and to accomplish things, but they don't want to be faithful first.

"Well you know, Pastor, I've got a ministry and there's an anointing on my life, too." Yes, but your character stinks! How do we know your character stinks? Because it's not that you're ignorant, you know better! Everybody knows that but you. Everybody's watching that but you.

And, of course, one of the biggest challenges is that people see *themselves* in light of their *intentions* and judge *other people* in light of their *actions*.

Let's say, for example, that Chuck did something to me. Chuck has hurt me in some way. I'm judging Chuck by what he *did*. I have no knowledge of his *intentions*. He knows his intentions, so he might be completely oblivious to the fact that he hurt me because his intentions were not to hurt me!

This happens all the time. You're running around upset with someone, and they don't even know why you're upset.

You're thinking, "Oh, they *know* what they did!" No, they don't, because they're judging the situation in light of what their intentions were, and you're judging it in light of their actions.

So faithfulness is often blurred in the lines of your intentions.

"Well, I didn't mean it that way!" Well, the truth of the matter is that the way you handled it (your actions) needed to line up with the way God wanted it handled. Your intentions should not supersede being responsible or being wise enough to guard yourself in how you handle the things God has asked you to do or the things you are involved in.

Paul said the power, the grace, and the miraculous ability came because he was counted faithful.

Do you know what "counting" means, in this context?

Counting is meant literally—like if I handed you a stack of money and you counted it. What is that doing? It's figuring out how much is really there, whether it's ten dollars or twenty dollars, a hundred dollars or a million dollars. You have to count it!

Paul said, "He *counted* me faithful." In other words, "He looked at all the situations and all the times of my life and said, 'He has been *counted.* Every time I've see him and done an accounting of him, he has been faithful.'"

Even if Paul was ignorant and didn't know the whole truth, he was faithful to what he *did* know. Nobody was out there killing Christians like Paul was! He was gettin' it!

People don't understand; flaky people are flaky! You have to help people to know sometimes that fat meat is greasy, if you know what I mean—because they don't know!

God is looking to enable people who are *faithful*. And if you're not faithful, why would God put His grace upon you to accomplish something that you refuse to do the way God wants it done? This is why marriages implode. I've seen relationships blow up because they're not doing it the way God said to do it. And then they're sitting back, praying—witchcraft!

Only witchcraft overrides the way God wants something done. If you think about the very nature of voodoo and witchcraft, it is to override what is supposed to be handled or done. So to pray over something that you know you are handling incorrectly—it's like people who don't tithe praying, "God bless me!" It doesn't make any sense.

I know this isn't popular, and many pastors don't talk about it, but it is very much truth, I assure you! And if you want to see the grace of God, if you want to see the empowerment of God, then you're gonna have to do things His way. As He counts you faithful, He increases you and gives you the ability to function in such a way that you are considered reliable, accurate, dependable, trustworthy, firm, dutiful, loyal, and so on.

Have you ever known somebody who only gives you half-answers whenever you ask them questions? You're like, "Seriously? You can't come up with a better, more accurate answer than that?"

Did you know that accuracy is a sign of faithfulness?

Loyalty is a sign of faithfulness. So many people in the body of Christ are disloyal, and they wonder why they struggle! Loyalty means you're committed even after the feeling you had at the moment in which you committed yourself has gone.

I come from a generation that was loyal. If you had a problem with somebody, then I had a problem with somebody. I don't play both sides of the fence. I'm not going to talk to you and then talk to the other person or say something different. If I say something about you, I'm going to say it *to* you!

Are people safe when they're not around you?

That's faithfulness! Faithful people handle things faithfully.

TITUS 2:9
Exhort servants to be obedient unto their own masters, and to please them well in all things; not answering again; Not purloining, but shewing all good fidelity; that they may adorn the doctrine of God our Saviour in all things.

Paul's talking to people who are in slavery, and he says, "For those of you in slavery, act like you've been taught; because everything you do shows a reflection on what you have been taught, and what our God teaches. Don't take things of small value... ."

You know how you sometimes find a nice pen that you like? You're like, "Ooh, I'm taking this!" That's not yours. You didn't pay for it, you didn't buy it.

"Well, you know, I just need a little bit of paper for my printer at home, so I'm just gonna take a little bit of paper from work. Nobody will miss it!"

He said, "Don't even take things of small value. Be *entirely* faithful and loyal, understanding that *God* is watching." He told slaves to deal with their masters as if they were dealing with God!

How you deal with even your boss is important. You know, the boss you don't like! The one you think is incompetent. The one you think doesn't like you. It's so significant, because here you want a raise. Here you want a better position. Here you want a promotion. But you sit around the water cooler saying things like, "Man, I can't believe how messed up the boss is. I can't believe how they talked to me. Don't they know I deserve more? I'm a child of the Most High God! I rebuke them!" You're sitting there gossiping.

Do you know what an ornament is? It sits on a tree; it's a decoration.

How many of you all know that a Christmas tree is designed as a backdrop for the ornaments? Nobody puts up a Christmas tree with nothing on it! *God wants you to stand out above everyone else.*

How do you handle yourself when you serve? Do you show up?

Do you show up *on time*?

Do you call at the last minute and say you can't make it, or send somebody a text message saying you won't be there today, and now everybody's got to scramble to try to cover for you?

What kind of ornament are you?

What do you represent when you do things like that?

How about your job? Are you dragging into work, late every day?

What kind of ornament are you?

Businesses, companies, executives—they'll put up with a lot of stupidity if you're faithful. They really will. Their tolerance for stupidity mitigates very quickly the less faithful you are, because their patience runs short! I've watched so many people struggle with jobs;

keeping jobs, going from job to job, and not realizing that the reason God's blessing hand is not on it is because they're not honoring Him in how they handle it. They're the first ones who've got some lip to say! And if anybody comes to them to talk bad about the company, or the organization, or the boss, they're the first one to listen and to hear that garbage instead of saying, "I don't wanna hear that, so take that junk somewhere else."

They're like, "Well, I won't make any friends that way." Well, those types of friends are the type you don't need!

Can God use you as an ornament on the tree?

Can people look at you and say, "I don't know what it is about them, but there's definitely something different"? Or are you always trying to find the shortest shortcut, the fastest way and the easiest way?

There's a meme out there that says something to the effect of, "The reward for me doing such a good job is that I get to do somebody else's work."

Even if that is the case for you, let me explain something. In every company where I ever worked, I made myself indispensable because I understood spreadsheet management. Working in an organization's C-levels, you learn very quickly what spreadsheet management is. The executives look at spreadsheets. They don't care about your commitment; they don't look at your family; they don't care how many bills you have to pay. They look at a spreadsheet with a name and a salary. And if they have to make budget, they start cutting.

So I began to realize something.

Years ago in a company I worked for, a guy (let's call him "John") was one of our engineers. He probably made about a quarter of a million dollars a year.

Now, our average engineer was making forty to sixty thousand a year!

I was the Chief Sales Officer, the CSO. We got on the call with the CEO (the Chief Executive Officer) and some of the directors, and they were all talking about this spreadsheet that just got emailed out, going down the list. Naturally, John's name was at the top of the list. Nobody brought his name up. They literally skipped number one and went to number two, number three, and so on and so forth.

Now, the reason they didn't talk about number one is because John was *the* best guy we had. Truthfully, he was probably one of the top people on the *planet;* that's how good he was. We'd send him into the worst situations. We once sent him to *Japan.* He flew all night, got off the plane, went into the law firm, fixed the problem, got back on a plane, flew back to Hawaii, fixed *their* problem there (same company!) and then flew back to DC and *never* slept.

Nobody discussed his salary! Nobody even discussed his usefulness, because he was faithful.

There have been times when I wanted to hire someone, and I would give them a task. I would tell them, "This is what I want you to do and this is how I want you to do it." You test them to see if they'll do things the way they are told, because what you need is *faithfulness.*

"Well, until you start paying me, I'm not going to be faithful."

We have names for people who will work only when they're paid. Or let me say it this way: We have names for people who will only *perform* when they're paid—none of which I'll repeat in this full gospel book!

Some people don't realize the reason why they don't get promoted is because they're just not faithful. They're too important in their own eyes. The empowerment, the enablement, the grace, the gifting doesn't show up because they're not faithful.

1 CORINTHIANS 4:2
Moreover it is required in stewards, that a man be found faithful.

There were times in my life when I don't know if I was tenacious or stupid. I'm just being honest. I don't know if I can say that I was always faithful in the sense that I understood what "faithful" meant and was diligent about being faithful. I think sometimes I was just dumb enough to not know anything else! Being focused was so important, and when God asked me to do something I just didn't know what else *to* do. So it was all I had.

1 Corinthians 4:2 tells us that there are moments in our lives when we are going to have to *prove*—not *say*, not *confess*—but to actually put ourselves in situations to show that we are, in fact, faithful.

These are people who go above and beyond the call of duty. They're reliable in everything. They tell you they're going to do something, and they do it. They tell you they're going to show up, and they show up. If you give them a project, they go above and beyond. That's why we don't use the term "volunteer" around here, because you'll never see the word "volunteer" in the Bible.

Let me tell you what volunteers look like, because some of you in your ministries have volunteers. You may not call them volunteers, but you have them! Those are the people who always tell you the time frame in which they can do something.

"Well, I can do that, but it has to be between this time and this time. It can't go over this time; I can't come before this time; I can only do it on this particular day." They know the church is open; they know the church needs them; they know that there's importance in what's going on; but they don't care because they're volunteers.

When you are not a volunteer, when you are a fervent servant, it's "What's needed? What do you need me to do? What do we need to do to get the end result? How do we get this thing accomplished?"

There's a whole different heart for someone who's a servant!

Now, listen, we need volunteers. But you have to think to yourself; how much grace is on volunteering?

What if God said, "I'll save you, but only so far"?

What if God was like, "Well listen, I know you need Me, but I'm going out tonight, so whatever you're praying about right now, you're going to have to hold it 'til Saturday morning!"

How you deal with God, and the things *concerning* God, is really the seed you're sowing as to how *you* are dealt with.

I get reports from all the ministry leaders at church: "So-and-so didn't show up; So-and-so didn't serve; So-and-so didn't show up and didn't even call." Invariably, So-and-so will end up in my office asking me if they can do more. You haven't been found faithful with what you've been given! How do you ask for more when you can't do the little stuff? This is the place where faithfulness is tested. This is where you are proving your faithfulness, proving your commitment!

People come in and out of our church, and I watch 'em. They'll come in, and they've got a ministry, and I know they have a ministry; I'm not stupid. I can sense by the Holy Ghost that they have a ministry. But what they want is for me to recognize their gift despite not having time to determine their character! I've seen many churches that are so desperate for people, they'll let somebody new come in and do anything they want to do, and then they'll wonder why their church is damaged, hurt, split, et cetera.

Here's what I've learned: You're not going to climb the ladder in this church if you don't even tithe to it. If you're not going to be committed to the organization God has placed you in, if you can't be committed to Him, you *definitely* ain't gonna be committed to me! If you don't have a fear of God, you *certainly* don't have respect for anything related to me. It's true! That's why our verse says you *prove* faithfulness, because when you prove it, there's a series of tests and moments where God expects you to be faithful. And it says that this is an *essential quality* of a steward.

What is a steward? Let's say I have a bottle of water. It is *my* bottle of water. If I give it to the guy next to me to hold it for me, he is now stewarding what belongs to me.

Now, can he drink it? No. Who does it belong to? *Me.*

So then he's not supposed to *partake* in what I've given him to steward, he's supposed to *protect it,* guard it, and multiply it. So when I give him one bottle, if he's faithful, he gives me back two. Now I call him faithful, because he increased what I gave him to steward.

Now, the beautiful thing about God is that He *allows* you to partake in what He gives you as long as you are faithful! People don't realize that nothing that they have actually belongs to them. And if you are not stewarding what *God* has given you to manage, it becomes "yours." The moment it becomes "yours," that's when it stops multiplying. That's why there's no increase, that's why there's no divine grace, that's why there's such a struggle.

PROVERBS 28:20
A faithful man shall abound with blessings: but he that maketh haste to be rich shall not be innocent.

What does *abound* mean? It means excess, right? Our verse says that "a faithful man shall *abound* with blessings, but he who makes haste to be rich at any cost shall not go unpunished."

So if someone is holding all that belongs to me—if he's holding it, if it's mine and he's a steward of it—if he's faithful? He could lose his job, his company could go under, his dog could bite him, his kids could act a fool, and he's still going to multiply it. Why?

Because he's talented?

Because he's handsome?

Because he's tall? Because he's short? Because he's gifted? Because he has money?

No, it's because he's *faithful.* So then, faithfulness becomes the currency! Faithfulness is *everything.*

I served under my pastor for almost nine years. I carried his bags; I was his armor-bearer. We didn't have to have conversations on what it meant to be an armor-bearer. The first thing I did was I bought a few books on it. I studied it, and I learned what it meant to be an armor-bearer for him. So when we traveled places, I made *sure* that everything he needed, I had. Now, he was an ex-boxer! So it wasn't like he *needed* someone to carry his things—he wasn't frail. But I understood what it meant to bring a supply, and I understood what it meant to serve. So I served faithfully for *nine years* before he launched me into ministry.

There were years where I gave $30,000–$40,000 yearly with my tithe! The only time I missed church was when he missed church, because I was with him! I taught in Bible college two nights a week. We had three services a week, and I served in all of them. I ran a real estate company. I was in the top one percent of the Southwest district —me, *personally,* in real estate. Never worked nights, never worked weekends. Didn't do open houses on Sundays. If a client asked me to do one on Sunday, I would tell them I wasn't gonna do it.

They'd be like, "Well, we'll find another realtor."

I'd be like, "Deuces!"

But I was in the *top one percent in the Southwest district.*

So then we planted the church I pastor now, and I wasn't making anything for the first eight or nine months, and then after that it was maybe a couple hundred bucks a month. God put me in a house—we ended up getting a 1,900-square-foot house for free for almost a year.

What I want you to understand is this: I didn't know what else *to* do but what God asked me to do. Yet He found a way to get the ravens to come and feed me. I'm talking about real faith!

When you are faithful, you have the confidence to know that in every situation you can say, "God has *got me*, 'cause I have been faithful! I refuse to allow the world to tell me what I am and am not going to do. I may have a job, I may not have a job, but God will call the ravens to fly by my house and drop off whatever it is I need because I trust and believe in Him, because he counted me faithful!"

By putting me in the ministry, God said, "I can trust him. He'll preach it whether people like it or not, whether there are three people in the room or thousands in the room. He's not moved by circumstances, job offers, things, stuff, money—"

I know how to pack this place out! I know exactly how to do it, and I could do it within three or four weeks. Not a chair in here would be empty. But God didn't tell me to do it that way. God has given me a vision of what He wants and how He wants it done, and size doesn't matter.

Growth matters—anything that isn't growing is dead. So we *should* be growing, but we should be growing and developing people to a place where they are fully committed to God, which is *exactly* what He wants. He doesn't want a bunch of part-time Christians fighting the full-time devil getting their butts whooped full-time! When you're faithful, you have the ability to trust and know that God said, "A faithful man shall abound."

Our company really took a dive right after 9/11 happened. We had clients in the World Trade Center; we had clients in the Pentagon. It hit us pretty hard. We were a government company, and it was tough. One of the guys who worked in the higher level of the organization was a pastor, though I didn't know he was a pastor at the time. As I was being laid off, he kept telling me, "You don't know the plans God has for you."

I remember thinking to myself, "Dude. Pay me my money, and don't tell me about plans anybody else has got for me, because I plan to whoop you right here and now if I don't get every nickel I'm owed!"

I had no idea. I had no idea of the course that set my life on. Was it tough? Yes, it was tough. But when you're faithful to the things God has asked you to do when He has a plan and purpose for your life, He will enable you to make it.

This is why so many people don't feel and experience the enablement to make it. They're just not faithful with what they have. If you can't rejoice in what you already have, you're not faithful. He doesn't bring more to people who respect Him less! Everything you have, He gave to you in the first place!

PROVERBS 25:19
Confidence in an unfaithful man in time of trouble is like a broken tooth, and a foot out of joint.

I don't know if you've ever had a broken tooth, but I think dentists are of the devil.

Nobody is excited to go see a dentist! If you are, you're just crazy!

(If any dentists are reading this, I'm just playing. I love all dentists! But seriously, nobody tries to have a need to go see a dentist.)

I once had a broken tooth pulled. So they gave me some medicine and some Ibuprofen, and I *hate* drugs. Of any form!

So I'm like, "You know what? I won't mess with this Ibuprofen. I'm not going to mess with this other medication. It's a prescription and it's an opiate, so I'm not gonna mess with that. I'm *tough*, I'm a *man*, baby, I'mma be all right!"

I didn't even get the prescription filled! That's how tough *I* was gonna be! This happened at about one o'clock.

By about 4 p.m., I was like "Honey? I'mma need you to go and fill this prescription."

So then I was like, "Here's what I'll do, I'll only take one or the other—but I won't take both!"

What I have subsequently learned, through that experience, is that the medication deals with *certain aspects* of the pain, and the Ibuprofen deals with the inflammation that causes a *different* type of pain!

So at about three o'clock in the morning, when I couldn't even sleep and my face was just *throbbing*, I came to the realization that I'd better just do what this doctor said!

I had to have a procedure done subsequently after that, and the first thing I told them to do was "Go ahead and send those prescriptions! Don't even give them to me. I need them electronically transmitted, and I need them to happen a lot faster than my little legs can carry them from one place to the next!"

I *immediately* left the dentist's office and went *straight* to the pharmacist and got these pills, and I took them before the pain *started* —because you might catch me once, but you ain't catchin' me twice!

The second experience was so much better than the first time!

A broken tooth is likened to a person who is unfaithful. That is the pain that person causes.

I don't know if you've ever had a broken foot, but a broken foot is *no joke*. It's hard to heal; you can't put any pressure on it; it completely alters your life.

The two most painful things—God says that when you're unfaithful, that's what you're like. It must be important!

Paul told Timothy, "The things I taught you, teach them to faithful men."

Do you know what he defined as *faithful*? He defined faithful as "Those who are able to teach others."

See, faithful people receive what God has, and they're able to impart it because they are faithful—they can be trusted with it.

Let's say that something I've said has nailed your hide to the wall. Here's how you know if your hide got nailed to the wall: It's like a cat. You know how they say "rub it the wrong way" or "rub it the right way"? What you've gotta do is turn the cat around or change the way you rub it, right?

Well, God is rubbing you the right way. So if the fur on your back is up, your hide's getting nailed! Now, you have two choices. You can say, "You know what? This is worthy; this is weighty; this is precious. God is revealing some things to me. I know it's the Word, so when I give it importance, I'm proving that I'm faithful. When I start walking in it, I'm proving that I'm faithful. Now I know I'm a candidate to abound."

Or you can keep being incredulous. You can keep acting like, "Oh, that was for somebody behind me," knowing the fur on your neck is *all* up. You're all fuzzed up, ready to blow up at any moment!

Years ago, I had a personal trainer, a professional bodybuilder. She had this little green bird, and when she said the words, "Bring it," he would literally puff up. All of his feathers would go *straight up in the air*—and he'd strut around saying, "Bring it! Bring it! Bring it!"

You know how I know people's hides are getting nailed to the wall?

When people start to look just like that little bird, all fuzzed up, going, "Bring it!"

It's better just to make the adjustments. Count these things as weighty.

The Marines have a motto: In Latin, it's "Semper Fidelis." Some say, "Semper Fi, Do or Die."

Do you know what "fidelis" means? It means *fidelity, faithfulness*. Their slogan means, in other words, "I'm either going to be faithful, or I'm going to die."

There is no in-between! It's not "Semper Fi, be flaky"! It's not "be indecisive"!

It's "Semper Fi, Do or Die."

Either we're going to be about the Father's business, or we're not. Because, if I can let you in on a little secret, I'd rather have 200 people in my church who are all going to heaven and whom I will know when I get there myself because the fruit has remained, than to have 13,000 and not see a single one in heaven. It is what it is—"Semper Fi, Do or Die." That's it. I don't have another choice, don't have any other options, don't have any other job or career I'm thinking about. I have businesses, and God will keep bringing me business as long as I keep this first. So I'm going to prosper, there's no question, because a faithful man abounds.

Another slogan of the Marines is "They run toward the sounds of chaos." *That's faithfulness*. That's fidelity. That's commitment. That's people who are not running from what needs to be done.

When you see tragedies and disasters happening on TV, you see First Responders running in the *opposite* direction everybody else is running in. That's why I have nothing but the utmost respect for those who serve as police, military, medical, emergency, and whatever it is that they do. If they make the commitment to run in the opposite direction of the one I'm running in to get away from chaos, that's faithfulness! That's when you make a decision, "I'm willing to lay my life down." And sometimes I can't even find people to fold a bulletin!

"I'm busy, Pastor, I've got stuff going on"—*Seriously?*

Semper Fi, Do or Die.

CHAPTER 9

INGRATITUDE

Let's return to 1 Samuel 2:29–35:

> Wherefore kick ye at my sacrifice and at mine offering, which I have commanded in my habitation; and honourest thy sons above me, to make yourselves fat with the chiefest of all the offerings of Israel my people? Wherefore the LORD God of Israel saith, I said indeed that thy house, and the house of thy father, should walk before me for ever: but now the LORD saith, Be it far from me; for them that honour me I will honour, and they that despise me shall be lightly esteemed. Behold, the days come, that I will cut off thine arm, and the arm of thy father's house, that there shall not be an old man in thine house. And thou shalt see an enemy in my habitation, in all the wealth which God shall give Israel: and there shall not be an old man in thine house for ever. And the man of thine, whom I shall not cut off from mine altar, shall be to consume thine eyes, and to grieve thine heart: and all the increase of thine house shall die in the flower of their age. And this shall be a sign unto thee, that shall come upon thy two sons, on Hophni and Phinehas; in one day they shall die both of them. And I will raise me up a faithful priest, that shall do according to that which is in mine heart and in my mind: and I will build him a sure house; and he shall walk before mine anointed for ever.

Faithfulness is a sign of honor unto God. Can you be depended upon,? Can you be trusted? Do you do things the way that is in God's heart and God's mind? Or do you have your own heart and mind on everything else? If it seems to fit, then you'll do it. If it doesn't seem to fit, then you'll just massage it into whatever you think you want it to be.

One thing becomes very apparent in this scripture: God had a plan for their lives, but they short-circuited the plan themselves!

You can short-circuit the plan God has for you. Just because you know the plan, just because you sense that there's a plan, just because you feel that there is a plan for your life—just because you feel it doesn't mean it is. There are some things that you have to do.

I think, sometimes, that we have this nature about when the world comes into what we believe. The world tries to convince us that God doesn't really care—and He does! The Bible says God is the same. God doesn't change. He's the same yesterday, today, and forever. So when you deal with God, you have to know God cares about how He's treated. God cares about how you handle the things He brings into your life.

The "I" of this chapter is INGRATITUDE.

Ingratitude is so significant if you want to walk in more revelation. If you want greater revelation in your life, this is where you want to start paying attention!

When I listen to the things Pastor Ricky Edwards will talk to me about, I often wonder "Where in the world did he get this from?" There have been times where he said something to me that I thought was heresy, I ain't gonna lie! He said it, and I'm like "Whatever. That doesn't even sound right, that doesn't make sense."

But you know, I was never stupid enough to say it out loud. One thing I'm smart enough to do is shut my mouth. And it's funny because now some of the things he tried to talk to me about and get me to understand *years* ago—some of them up to ten years ago—I finally get today. But it took some time!

So I want you to understand that when things are handled properly according to what's in God's heart and mind, you will find yourself walking in greater degrees of light. And when we walk in greater degrees of light, then we qualify for more light.

> **DEUTERONOMY 29:29**
> **The secret things belong unto the LORD our God: but those things which are revealed belong unto us and to our children for ever, that we may do all the words of this law.**

How are we able to push or to force revelation?

We're not able. You can't force God to move. What you can do is set an atmosphere for revelation.

One of the biggest mistakes, the most amateur thing some ministers will do is they'll try to *force* God to move. So you find churches with fog machines, trying to make it look like the fog has rolled in. Listen, I have been in churches where the fog has rolled in, and it wasn't a fog machine! I'm all about the *real* Presence of God. We've had services at our church where the fog has rolled in! When it's genuine, that's what I want. If it ain't genuine, I don't want anything to do with it because it's counterfeit. I want it done the way that's in God's heart and mind.

However, what we can do—by our participation, by our desire, by our earnest pull, we can create an atmosphere in which God *can* move. We will never be able to force God to move, but we can create an atmosphere in our life in which He is *able* to move.

If you struggle with your attitude, if you're like, "Well, this is just who I am, and I am what I am"—No, if you're a jerk, then you're just a jerk. You'll be praying, asking God to move in your life and your situation, and yet you are resentful, you are angry, you haven't set an atmosphere for God to move in!

That's why the Bible says that "Faith worketh by love."[28] Faith explodes by love! There is no possible way for God to move in a situation when you can't walk in love.

"Well, I don't like the way they talk to me." So what? Your prayers are falling to the ground like lead balloons!

There's a way, there's a pattern, there's an understanding of how if you want to create the atmosphere that God can move in. So you're going to have to create that atmosphere and do it by faith.

You cannot force revelation, but you can create an atmosphere *for* revelation. So how I handle what's been revealed to me will determine what continues to belong to me.

Did you know that we are raising the most biblically illiterate generation?

"Well, I don't want to force them to go to church; my parents forced me to go to church." Yeah? Well, guess what? Some things are non-negotiable. It's like getting washed (I hope you were forced to get washed when you were a kid!)

I don't get the logic behind people thinking it's not their responsibility to spend the time to invest what belongs to us into our children. It belongs to us forever for what reason? *So that we may do exactly that.*

Because we don't have the transference of what's been revealed, we have a lack of revelation. Kids are not walking in the revelation we used to have because our parents took time to put the fear of God in us so that we would understand what is right and wrong, that everything is not like a video game.

---

[28] Galatians 5:6.

You see all these action heroes and superheroes dying in the movies, but next thing you know they're on television, alive, getting an award. It teaches kids that there are no permanent consequences for their actions! People run around killing people in video games, but if you don't like what's going on, just hit the reset button and it will start all over. Ain't no reset button in life!

So you have to understand that whatever has been revealed to you, what you do with it will determine your level of gratitude. Ingrates are not grateful, they are not appreciative. When things are revealed, God expects you to appreciate what's been revealed! And when it's been revealed to you, you shouldn't have a problem sharing it!

You get a new car—the car you've been waiting for, the car you've been dreaming about. The first thing you want is for everybody to see it. You pull up to somebody's house; you park right in front, park halfway across their front lawn just so you know that when they come to the door, they're gonna see it! You're so proud of it, you're so excited about it!

If God reveals something to you about how to *get* that car, then you have nothing to say.

Do you see what's been revealed as valuable?

Whatever you don't transform, you will transfer. Whatever is valuable to you, your kids will know.

My child does not have a cognitive understanding of what a phone is. Has no idea what it is, what it does, what it's supposed to do, how it's made, how it works or functions. She has no clue! But tell me why she can grab it and put it up to her ear, tell me why she wants it so badly. Because she sees me using it so much.

You'll transfer what's important to you. So the question becomes this: Is what God has revealed to you important enough to transfer it to your children?

PSALMS 25:14
The secret of the LORD is with them that fear him;
and he will shew them his covenant.

You mean to tell me that if I'm honorable, and I revere God, and I respect the things of God, then secrets that He has will begin to be revealed to me? And that He will show me His covenant?

So if I am not able to see and/or experience the things that come from His covenant, then I have to ask myself: If the things He's trying to show me seem to be elusive and secretive to me, then do I fear Him (and by that I don't mean afraid, I mean a reverential awe)? Do I honor Him?

When we begin to understand the importance of honoring God and are grateful for Him and the things He reveals, and for the covenant He's given us, He begins to show us the deep things concerning His covenant—the depth of which none of us fully knows!

Lately, I have started seeing some things God has been revealing to me concerning certain positions people have. For example, I have noticed that when people struggle with—let's say a minister owning a jet or a plane—it's really bizarre to me how people struggle with that level of functioning! But a CEO who sells sugar water—they have no problem with that person having a jet.

If I'm called to do greater things, then my level of function, revelation, and prosperity has to be different than yours. If you are called to reach a city and I'm called to reach the world, how am I going to do that riding on the back of a donkey? Unless that donkey's a real good swimmer!

This means that different people have different responsibilities and different functions, and accordingly, it is likely that they walk in different revelations. So a person who can believe God for ten million dollars a month is not walking in the same revelation as somebody who can believe God for ten dollars a month—not that there's anything wrong with it, but it's not my place to judge it! It's not my place to even speak on it; it's none of my business. Who am I to judge another man's servant?

If I have a calling or a purpose on my life, then I have to be clear on the level of revelation I walk in. More importantly, I've got to make sure that I am open to the revelation I need to walk in in order to have what I need to have.

To put it differently: Some people I know are extremely anointed and God has a call on their life and has an extreme purpose for them— and not just in rhetoric! Yokes will be broken and bondage will be destroyed in their ministry, and I know for a fact that God has great things for them to do. I also know that they need to understand early on—now—because of the call on their life, who they marry makes a difference. While it might not make a difference to someone who is not called to their level, the level to which they are called requires that they cannot marry Mr. or Mrs. Right Now. If they get married to the wrong person for the wrong reasons, their revelation is not there. And because the revelation is not there, God cannot show them to the level that He could if they would walk in, regard, and honor Him. It's basic, it's simple.

How we got away from this, I do not know. But the more honor and regard you have for God and the things associated with God, the more growth you will find in that. You will find that God will give you greater and greater revelations and understanding because He is showing you His covenant—not your perception of it, but the fullness of what He has for you!

ROMANS 11:33
O the depth of the riches both of the wisdom and knowledge of God! how unsearchable are his judgments, and his ways past finding out!

In other words: Who told God all the stuff that God knows?

Do you have any idea of the depth of what God wants to take us to?

Sometimes people say, "Well, you know, I didn't appreciate how So-and-so handled something. I hired them to do a job and they didn't do a good job, so I feel like I shouldn't pay them."

Now they're fighting over money.

"Well, if they'd done the job right, I would have paid them!"

How about we insert this thought: If you'd been led by the Holy Ghost, you wouldn't have hired that idiot in the first place! See, you have no idea how deep God can go in His leadership of your life. Because of that, you limit God to your level of understanding.

So many people want to put God on their level.

"I can't believe God let me down, and God did this." No, no, Honey Boo-Boo.

God ain't on your level! And if you missed it, then own up, put your big boy pants on, and realize that *you* missed it and now it's *your* job to figure out how to get it back to where it was supposed to be in the first place. It is not God's responsibility to step into your level of revelation. He is not showing you *a* covenant, He is showing you *His* covenant. And if He's showing you *His* covenant, then you have *no idea* what He can do for you!

I've heard people say, "Well, Pastor, the reason why I don't tithe is because I'm on a fixed income." Who fixed it? Your mouth? Your confession? How are you ever going to prosper if you're constantly asking people for something?

PROVERBS 25:2
It is the glory of God to conceal a thing: but the honour of kings is to search out a matter.

God does not hide things from you.

He hides things *for* you.

And because people tend to be so lazy, they don't value revelation, they don't value their growth, they don't value the Word of God, they don't value their church attendance. Listen, faith doesn't come by *heard*, faith comes by hear*ing*.

There is a ministry of hearing, there is a ministry of The Word, there's a ministry of preaching and teaching. Why? So that you continue to walk in light, and receive light, and grow in the things of God. *But it is your responsibility to search it out.*

So many people want me to give them the revelation.

"Pastor, can I just sit in your office and you just give it to me?" No! I cannot.

It is *your* responsibility to get off of your *Como Se Llama*, get off of your John Brown Hind Parts, and do the things that you're supposed to do to search out a matter so that you begin to seek into this matter. God will begin to speak to you about what it is that He's trying to say and how He's trying to say it.

My job is to come and bring my little food and say, "Here's what I've got; let me feed you." But if you aren't getting full, you ain't eating! It's really that simple.

When I begin to talk to people, I can always identify people who are dry as *Shuck*. They don't study their Bible; they don't have devotional time; they don't read for themselves. All they do is go from service to service hoping they get what it is that they need. And because they do not spend the time it takes to search out a matter—because God hid it on purpose—God wants to know, "Are you gonna come after this, or are you thinking I'm just going to give it to you?"

Are you going to go after and search out a matter and get revelation? Are you hungry for it? Do you really want it so badly that you are hot after His trail?

As He begins to see that you are chasing very closely, then He says, "I've gotta give him some handfuls of purpose; I've gotta give her some things because she is after it, and I will always respond to the hungry."

It is not about the intelligent; it's about *who is hungry* after the things of God. Because when you begin to search out a matter, it is the honor of God to conceal it and the honor of kings to go get it.

What doesn't make sense to you today will never make sense to you if you don't treat it as valuable.

"Lord, I don't know what you're telling me, but I know this is important, so your servant is listening."

Why do you have to tell Him, "I'm listening"? *Honor.*

Teenagers—they think they have all the answers to all the wrong questions, right? They're teenagers, so they know it all. And you can tell when they're not listening! But what happens when you start talking and your child says, "I'm listening"? It's a whole different level of respect and honor.

You want God to speak to you, but you give Him zero opportunity for Him to do so because you machine-gun your prayers, like, "Lord—letmetellyouallthethingsIneed, letmetellyouwhatI'vegottado, IhavethisproblemI'vegottatellyouabout, solistenI'lltalktoyoulaterbye!"

God's like, "I already know what you need. I know what you know."

So people think, "Oh well, I'll just make an appointment with Pastor and I'll ask him!"

You have been disobedient with all that you've already heard! It wasn't important; it wasn't significant.

God revealed stuff to you and you were like, "Oh, that was good!" *Did you write it down?* Nope!

Sitting in the middle of service, you've *got* it. "Oh my *God*, that was it *right there!" But did you write it down*? Nope!

So of course, two days later, you're in the middle of a situation that revelation could have helped you with. But because you didn't think it was important enough to write down, it can't help you!

> **1 JOHN 1:6–7**
> **If we say that we have fellowship with him, and walk in darkness, we lie, and do not the truth: But if we walk in the light, as he is in the light, we have fellowship one with another, and the blood of Jesus Christ his Son cleanseth us from all sin.**

Let's say I get a revelation that "water is wet."

When I begin to really study water and its wetness, I start to walk in the light I was given. So now I can qualify for more light if I'm willing to walk in the light I have.

There are a lot of Facebook prophets out there. They have Facebook revelations, but they walk in none of it themselves. How do you know? Because you can see their life.

That's why Paul said, "I don't want to preach to others and myself become a castaway."

Half the people I've met who told me they were a pastor shouldn't have been one. They're a pastor because they found an application online and sent it in. They're a pastor somehow because they got offended by another pastor and decided they were going to start their own church—which is, by the way, exactly how Satan started.

You can't walk in darkness and claim to have light. You have to come out of the darkness that you're in in order to walk in light, in order to get more light. And so many people don't understand that the reason that they're not getting light is because they're walking in darkness. They have chosen, by their incredulousness, to walk in darkness.

They're praying, "God, reveal to me the next business investment to make, reveal to me the next deal to do." And they're so dishonorable with everything else, walking in darkness, and wondering where the light is! And that's where Satan comes in and gets them to question *all of it.*

How do you know if you're walking in light? You're fellowshipping one with another. *Fellowship* means there's a commonality, an exchanging of support and effort. There are deeper things that go into fellowship other than just hanging out.

How do you know when people are not walking in light? They don't want to have fellowship.

"Well, I don't need church." Okay! We'll see how that works out for you!

If there wasn't something about it, why would Paul tell his fellowship to throw the man who slept with his father's wife out of the church? He could turn him over to Satan without throwing him out, couldn't he? *No.*

But people turn *themselves* over to Satan.

How do they do that? They pull themselves out of fellowship. Then you see them on Facebook with a drink in their hand, slowly working themselves out of fellowship and into darkness. But they'll post on Facebook all these quotes on how God revealed stuff to them —God didn't reveal a thing.

Jehovah ain't revealed a thing, *Adonai* has not revealed a thing— the god of *This World*, who comes *masquerading* as an angel of light, has revealed a lot of things.

You cannot walk in darkness and receive light.

Let me put it in a practical way: You're single. Boy meets girl, girl meets boy. Boy is now sleeping with girl, girl is now sleeping with boy.

Boy now prays, "God, reveal to me if she is the one." What are you talking about? That horse has left the gate already!

Girl prays, "Lord, take him away if he's not supposed to be in my life." You have walked in darkness, and now you want some light!

You want light? Drop him. Drop her. Back away from the situation. Repent unto God. And *then* say, "Okay, *now* show me what's going on. I have come out of the darkness; now I can get some light because now that I'm in light and I know what this is, now I qualify for more light."

But what light is going to come into the darkness you're walking in? Especially darkness you *chose*!

Contrary to what people may want you to think, nobody "accidentally" sleeps with somebody. You don't just fall in —"Whoops!" No, that's not how that happens. There's planning involved; there's scheduling involved; there's the disrobing of all of your clothes involved; there are a lot of things that have to transpire to make that jump off! When Adam and Eve were rockin' around naked, it was a little easier—still ain't gonna fall into the situation, but it was a little easier!

People have no idea! When they choose to walk in darkness, somehow they think God is responsible.

PROVERBS 4:18
But the path of the just is as the shining light, that shineth more and more unto the perfect day.

Nobody's got all the revelations. We're all working toward a place of the perfect day, the maturity of the perfect light. You will never have all of the light or the perfect light until you get up to heaven. Until then, you're constantly growing and maturing, taking steps in your righteousness. That's why the Bible says we are righteous as He is righteous.

In other words, we begin to develop and grow as we begin to compare ourselves to Christ—nobody else!

"Well, at least I haven't slept with as many guys as Kimber did!" That does not matter! Because the truth of the matter is if Kimber doesn't have any light on the subject, and *you do*?

Stop searching after stuff that you don't have an answer for, and start walking in the light that you *do* have, that you *have* an answer for, that *has* been revealed to you, and walk in *that*.

One of the fastest and quickest signs that a person has a bad spirit, particularly the spirit of Jezebel, is they are *only* nice to Pastor— nobody else! They can't seem to find common ground with anybody else, so they are baiting for opportunities to be close to the pastor. They're coyly nice to the first lady, too, because what they're trying to do is gain influence. What it shows, by their behavior, is that they're really walking in darkness. So it's always the Jezebels who have the greatest and latest revelation of what they call light.

PROVERBS 4:19
The way of the wicked is as darkness: they know not
at what they stumble.

Notice what it says: They stumble. They're tripping and falling, but they don't know over what. So they want to make appointments with everybody so they can be told what it is, because they don't know what it is! Why don't they know what it is? Because it's in darkness.

How do you deal with things that are in darkness? You've got to turn on the light.

Most of us have learned that as we get older, the frequency of our bathroom trips increases. In the middle of the night, when I'm at home, there is no problem! I can navigate with no light, because I've done it a thousand times. But if I'm in unfamiliar territory, now I'm in stub-toe country! I'm trying to figure out where I'm going and how to get there in an expedient amount of time before the circumstance changes! I don't know what I'm stumbling over until I turn the light on. But if *I'm* the one who refuses to turn the light on?

You know you're supposed to walk in love, right?

"Yeah, well, I'm angry." Oh.

"You don't understand what I've been through." Oh.

One time a lady came up to Pastor Ricky, and she wanted to be prayed for. When he went to lay hands on her, the Lord told him not to. He wasn't clear why not, so the Lord told him, "She's dealing with unforgiveness—she's just mean."

So he asked her, "Ma'am, is there somebody or something you're supposed to be forgiving, and you're really not?"

And she said, "Just lay your hands on me so I can get healed!"

He said, "You can take your crippled self back and sit down!"

Some of you may think, "Wow, that was really harsh." You're right! But if she wants to get healed?

He brought light. God revealed it to him, he revealed it to her, he brought light. She turned out the light switch. So what's the point? He can lay hands on her until he rubs the hair smooth off her head—she's made the decision to walk in darkness, so she's just stumbling over herself. He turned the light on, and she clicked it right back off. There's nothing he could do for her.

I'm up at 4 a.m. every day. If I go to bed at 3:30 a.m., I'm up at 4 a.m. I'm wired that way. Sometimes I can sleep late—until about 5 a.m. And that is a *late morning*. Now, I don't go around turning on lights. My wife is still asleep. I've been able to negotiate how to get out of the room—I grab the door very quietly; I can go through it and close it without slamming it. She can stay asleep. She gets up at about 5–5:30 a.m. I give her that hour and a half. I don't go turning on the lights because light is progressive—if you turn it on all at once, it shocks the system, and you're looking around and you can't see because your eyes aren't used to the light yet.

Light is revealed progressively. God gives you a little light here; once you walk in that, you get a little more.

The day you decide to walk in love, the first thing that's going to happen is your dog won't bite you, your spouse won't act stupid, you're gonna get in the car, drive down the street, somebody's gonna tell you you're Number 1, you're gonna get to work and everybody at work's gonna be acting stupid, because you decided to walk in love!

If the dog bites you, "It's okay, Fido."

If your wife's getting on your nerves, "Honey, it's all right, I love you. Did I ever tell you how pretty your eyes are?"

You get in the car, somebody cuts you off and shows you you're Number 1, and you're like, "Thank you for telling me I'm Number 1; I so appreciate that!"

And then you get to work, and you're like, "I'm not gonna put up with none of this crap! Not near another minute!"

The light was on for a minute, at least! You master that; you take another step and you master that; and you take another step, and so on and so forth. And as you move, light is shining, and shining, and shining more and more until a perfect day comes.

At 4 a.m., the sun is not up. At 5 a.m., the sun is not up. It starts coming up between about 6 and-7 a.m. It gradually rises into a perfect day, and it begins to reveal itself. It doesn't just pop up and go, "Hey, I'm here!" The day dawns, and light begins to grow and change and develop, and this is the way things work in you!

God is trying to get you into deeper things and deeper revelations, but if you can't even love your neighbor, sit down—take several seats —and shut up! You're talking about "I want the deeper things of God,

I wanna go to a church where I can hear some deep things." *You* ain't deep! You can't even get the basic concepts straight! You can't show up, you can't attend, you can't tithe, you can't seem to serve, but you want the *deep things of God*, the *revelations*!

A perfect day starts with the things you don't appreciate, because you're ungrateful for that which He did reveal to you. And because you're an ingrate over what He did reveal to you, stop asking for more, because you won't value that either!

"Pastor, if I knew what I was called to do, I would do it." No you wouldn't! If you can't do what you were told to do, you darn sure ain't gonna do what you were called to do!

"Well, I beg to differ; I think I would." Well, who cares? If you can't write a tithe check for two dollars, you won't write one for two million.

People crack me up with their way of thinking and their way of functioning. They just think God is okay when He's not.

ISAIAH 28:9–10
Whom shall he teach knowledge? and whom shall he make to understand doctrine? them that are weaned from the milk, and drawn from the breasts. For precept must be upon precept, precept upon precept; line upon line, line upon line; here a little, and there a little.

In this passage, the "drunkards of Ephraim" are saying, "They're talking to us like we're little kids! Are we just weaned from our mothers' breasts? Are we just little babies?"

And Isaiah prophesies with God's response, "How do I know you're a little baby? Because you're still sucking on a bottle, on the binky of encouragement! I cannot give you the deeper things because line must be upon line, and precept upon precept. You're acting like a child, so I'm talking to you like children."

He said, "The only way I can give you the deeper things is if you put the binky down and master that! Then I can build a line and a precept on it."

Anything that you won't allow to be truth in your life, God can't build on. And in that area, you're still a baby. And then you wonder why you keep getting spoken to like a child, because you want the *Deep Stuff of God*.

> **MATTHEW 13:45–46**
> **Again, the kingdom of heaven is like unto a merchant man, seeking goodly pearls: Who, when he had found one pearl of great price, went and sold all that he had, and bought it.**

What happens when the things of the Kingdom are revealed to you?

Do you treat them as pearls of great price? Are you appreciative?

> **MATTHEW 7:6**
> **Give not that which is holy unto the dogs, neither cast ye your pearls before swine, lest they trample them under their feet, and turn again and rend you.**

If you give a hungry dog something inedible to eat, it's gonna spit out that thing and come after you instead for not resolving its hunger.

Pearls are sacred things. God reveals certain things to you, and He says, "Do not take holy things and give them to dogs and swine." In other words, don't give God's precious holy things to people who are unable to discern the value and the importance of what's been given to you.

God has told me certain things that I wouldn't share with anyone but maybe my spiritual father, and some other things with only my wife. You wanna know why? Because I don't trust everybody! Because I'm not going to cast pearls, things of great price, before people who have no understanding of them. Because the moment they don't see the value in those things, they will turn and attack—because they don't see the value; not that there *isn't* value.

Pearls were *way* more valuable back in Jesus' day than they are today. But are pearls of great price? Yes, they are. So how come swine don't know it?

Let's say I treat what has been revealed to me as a pearl of great price—and the same thing could have been revealed to you! I saw it as the pearl it actually was, but you saw it as an inedible object because you were running around in a slop pen. But it was the same pearl! The difference is in the person receiving it, in the revelation of the individual who sees the pearl. It's all about what you value, what you consider to be of great price.

It's time for us to live in light, to appreciate the light we have, to see it as precious, and to walk in it.

CHAPTER 10

IDLENESS

Let's re-examine 1 Samuel 2:29–35:

Wherefore kick ye at my sacrifice and at mine offering, which I have commanded in my habitation; and honourest thy sons above me, to make yourselves fat with the chiefest of all the offerings of Israel my people? Wherefore the LORD God of Israel saith, I said indeed that thy house, and the house of thy father, should walk before me for ever: but now the LORD saith, Be it far from me; for them that honour me I will honour, and they that despise me shall be lightly esteemed. Behold, the days come, that I will cut off thine arm, and the arm of thy father's house, that there shall not be an old man in thine house. And thou shalt see an enemy in my habitation, in all the wealth which God shall give Israel: and there shall not be an old man in thine house for ever. And the man of thine, whom I shall not cut off from mine altar, shall be to consume thine eyes, and to grieve thine heart: and all the increase of thine house shall die in the flower of their age. And this shall be a sign unto thee, that shall come upon thy two sons, on Hophni and Phinehas; in one day they shall die both of them. And I will raise me up a faithful priest, that shall do according to that which is in mine heart and in my mind: and I

will build him a sure house; and he shall walk before mine anointed for ever.

We can see very clearly that the more honor we have toward God and toward the things of God, the greater the revelation we walk in and the greater the manifestation we receive. Because God is all about honor. One of the challenges we see here is that Eli didn't correct his sons. He did absolutely nothing, he let their disobedience go.

Remember Job—not only did Job correct his children, but he also made sacrifices for his children.

Job led his family in an honorable way, and Eli did nothing.

Sometimes people think that doing nothing is okay, when doing nothing is definitely not okay. So this chapter's "I" is IDLENESS—or in other words, *laziness*.

MATTHEW 25:14–29
For the kingdom of heaven is as a man travelling into a far country, who called his own servants, and delivered unto them his goods. And unto one he gave five talents, to another two, and to another one; to every man according to his several ability; and straightway took his journey. Then he that had received the five talents went and traded with the same, and made them other five talents. And likewise he that had received two, he also gained other two. But he that had received one went and digged in the earth, and hid his lord's money. After a long time the lord of those servants cometh, and reckoneth with them. And so he that had received five talents came and brought other five talents, saying, Lord, thou deliveredst unto me five talents: behold, I have gained beside them five talents more. His lord said unto him, Well done, thou good and faithful servant: thou hast been faithful over a few things, I will make thee ruler over many things: enter thou into the joy of thy lord. He also that had received two talents came and said, Lord, thou deliveredst unto me two talents: behold, I have gained two other talents beside them. His lord said unto him, Well done, good and

faithful servant; thou hast been faithful over a few things, I will make thee ruler over many things: enter thou into the joy of thy lord. Then he which had received the one talent came and said, Lord, I knew thee that thou art an hard man, reaping where thou hast not sown, and gathering where thou hast not strawed: And I was afraid, and went and hid thy talent in the earth: lo, there thou hast that is thine. His lord answered and said unto him, Thou wicked and slothful servant, thou knewest that I reap where I sowed not, and gather where I have not strawed: Thou oughtest therefore to have put my money to the exchangers, and then at my coming I should have received mine own with usury. Take therefore the talent from him, and give it unto him which hath ten talents. For unto every one that hath shall be given, and he shall have abundance: but from him that hath not shall be taken away even that which he hath.

How did the master determine how many talents each person's got? *By their ability.*

In other words, God gave each person the talents or the skillsets or whatever He has invested in them—the gifts He gave them—based on His perception of the ability of the individual receiving them. So we have to understand that no matter how *you* view what you have doesn't matter, because God viewed it a certain way, and He viewed it as important enough to give it to you. Now you have a responsibility to be responsible for your ability.

In our scripture, when the one who had been given five talents came back with five more, the Lord essentially said, "Well done, you have done this the way that was in My heart and in My mind. You have been faithful, so now enter into the joy of the Lord."

When the one who had been given two talents came back with two more, the Lord didn't say, "You should've done what the other one did and come back with five more." He said, "The things that I have given you, you have handled the way that is in My heart and My mind; you have been honorable and faithful toward Me. I don't expect you to do more than what I gave you to do. I don't expect you to have a five-talent return—I only gave you two! I expect you to do something with the two I gave you. If I had given you five, I would've expected you to do something with the five I gave you."

So then God's praise of these servants is not specific to the outcome; it is relative to the effort.

The guy who had 1 talent and hid it in the earth came back and said, "Here's your one talent back."

He was lazy! The Lord called him lazy!

He called himself *smart*. In his reasoning and the vain imagination of his own mind, he had a plan: "This man is very hard to deal with, so I'm gonna go ahead and hide His talent, and then when He comes back for it, I'm going to give Him back what He gave me." He's smart, in his own mind!

God called him *wicked and lazy*. He said "You should have taken what I gave you and at *minimum* put it into a savings account and left it there so I could draw some interest on the money I gave you. That way, when I came back, you wouldn't just be handing back to Me what I gave to you."

God expected him to do something with the talent He had blessed him with and to make gain—to increase it. He didn't expect him to increase it at the level of other people's increase, because you can't compare yourself to each other. Some people have got it, and some people don't. God sees some people as having a greater ability, and some people as not. It is what it is. So I want you to understand that He's talking about at least doing the *minimum* with what God has given you.

God said, "Instead of going out there and making something happen, you hedged your bet by thinking you would just give Me back something I gave to you."

Whatever God gives you, He doesn't want it back the way He gave it to you! If there's a gift in or on your life, He wants you to improve that gift and bring honor to Him by expanding or improving upon the very thing He gave to you. He doesn't want it back the same way you got it.

MATTHEW 25:28
Take therefore the talent from him, and give it unto him which hath ten talents.

With this idea of he who has and he who has not, Jesus is saying here that if the "person who has not" does not produce with what little he was given, God will take it from him and give it to the one who does have. All of society purports the idea that if you are successful, it is your obligation to give to those who are not. Yet in the Bible, Jesus tells this story and says, "If you don't handle what you have properly, we'll take that from you and give it to the one who has ten talents."

My success level with what I have entitles me to more.

So many people are like, "Well, I think that if you have money, you should take care of the poor and you should do this for me. You have it, so why don't you help me?"

Why don't you help yourself?

The truth of the matter is that it starts with you. And if you would be faithful with what you have, you would find greater success. But for so many people, because they're lazy about what they have, what they have keeps getting taken away.

And then they're like, "I'm praying to God, bless me!"

PROVERBS 6:6–11
Go to the ant, thou sluggard; consider her ways, and be

wise: Which having no guide, overseer, or ruler, Provideth her meat in the summer, and gathereth her food in the harvest. How long wilt thou sleep, O sluggard? when wilt thou arise out of thy sleep? Yet a little sleep, a little slumber, a little folding of the hands to sleep: So shall thy poverty come as one that travelleth, and thy want as an armed man.

What does this passage tell you? It tells you that what you won't do today is the reason why you'll starve tomorrow! When you are lazy about the things that need to get done, you should know that life functions in a rhythm.

One of the greatest challenges husbands and wives face is getting into the same rhythm. It's a cadence. It's "Are we moving together, are we stepping together?" A three-legged race is not won by those who are the fastest. It's won by those who are in cadence together. They can stay in-step with each other, and because of that, they can move faster than everybody else. If my partner is trying to move at a certain pace and I'm moving at a different pace, we're gonna have a fight! What is required is for us to be in sync with each other, so that as we move, we move together.

Life has a rhythm! And if you don't understand the rhythm of life, you will always be on the outside looking in, trying to figure out why you don't have what you need. And it'll be because you didn't do what you were supposed to do to get what you needed in the time that you needed it! You missed your timing.

Back in the days when cars had spark plugs, and the spark plugs had to be set to ten degrees before top dead center, and different cars had different settings—if that thing didn't fire when it was supposed to fire, that car ain't moving! The timing was everything. With the rotating of the engine, every fire had to spin it back around again, and it happened in fractions of a second! The timing was extremely significant, the timing could not be off or else that car wouldn't move.

In high school, I took "Engine Class." Everyone had to take apart an engine then put it back together. The final exam was that you had to put some gas in your engine and fire it up. If the engine fired up, then you passed the class.

I did not pass the class.

The engine *I* had to put together—this will tell you how old I am—had *breakpoints*.

Not even spark plugs!

I want you to understand the significance of cadence and timing. The reason why people struggle with themselves financially is that they do not plan *today* for what inevitably will happen tomorrow. They have not learned how to find the rhythm. There's a rhythm of investing, a rhythm of saving, a rhythm of spending—and if you don't learn how to do those things, if you are too lazy to figure this out, you will always be out of step, you will always have a shortage somewhere, you will always operate in lack, because it's dishonorable to God not to understand how these things work.

No matter what kind of pay increase I've ever gotten, I have never gotten a pay increase and then gone out and spent it all. I've allowed my life to catch up to where I needed to be, so that I did not go out and create a whole bunch of expenses and then cause myself to not be able to pay my bills.

I get so frustrated dealing with people who think they're honorable but don't pay their bills. You cannot be honorable when you have not paid your bills! You have put damage on other people and other organizations. The Bible says to render honor to whom honor is due, and to whom money is due, *pay them what you owe them*. When you live a lifestyle of honor, when you begin to understand honor, you begin to see things a little differently.

So when people are like, "I need a handout; can I borrow this and can I get this?" Listen, if you don't have enough money for the month, you spent too much. It's really simple.

It's like losing weight. The truth of the matter is that losing weight is based on a very simple combination—you must burn more energy than you eat. That's it!

If you want to be profitable, you must make more money than you spend. But our society has learned to live off of credit, so we get into a place where we live above our means. We just throw it on credit. What credit does is it breaks your rhythm in your cycle.

There is a rhythm and a cadence to life, a time for sowing seed and a time to harvest. We've got to understand that and prepare accordingly.

> **Matthew 12:36**
> **But I say unto you, That every idle word that men shall speak, they shall give account thereof in the day of judgment.**

Do you know what *idle* means?

It means *useless*. It means *lazy*. It means *doesn't do anything*. It has no power behind it, it's idle.

God is going to call you into account for every idle thing that doesn't have a purpose to it!

> **1 TIMOTHY 5:7–8**
> **And these things give in charge, that they may be blameless. But if any provide not for his own, and specially for those of his own house, he hath denied the faith, and is worse than an infidel.**

There is nothing worse than laziness. I think laziness is a disease— I really do! If you are able-bodied and you don't have a job, there's something wrong with that. And to watch your family struggle!

"Well, I'm looking for a job, Pastor" Well, you're not looking very hard!

We have a responsibility to bring a supply to our own household, so we can take care of the things we need to take care of. God considers it dishonorable to not do that. He says to treat people who don't do that as *worse* than an unbeliever! An unbeliever doesn't know any better; a believer *should* know better.

God said He'll bless the work of your hands, not the seat of your pants!

The Bible says if you don't work, you don't eat.

LUKE 13:6–9
He spake also this parable; A certain man had a fig tree planted in his vineyard; and he came and sought fruit thereon, and found none. Then said he unto the dresser of his vineyard, Behold, these three years I come seeking fruit on this fig tree, and find none: cut it down; why cumbereth it the ground? And he answering said unto him, Lord, let it alone this year also, till I shall dig about it, and dung it: And if it bear fruit, well: and if not, then after that thou shalt cut it down.

In other words, "If it doesn't produce, get rid of it. Why should it sit around and deplete everybody else?"

The gardener says, "Let me work on it a little bit longer! Let me see if I can get it to not be so lazy and produce."

These stories are told by our Master, who is helping us understand how He feels and how He regards a lack of production, a lack of productivity, a lack of producing. Yet we want to say that the rich should give to the poor, and the rich should be punished because they have done what the poor will not do! People want to lay it on you, make you feel guilty because you're doing well.

"Well, Pastor, you're driving this kind of car!" Yeah, I know.

My first car was a Ford Escort. When I moved to Arizona, I had a Honda Accord. I didn't start out with a nice car, and even if I did, then bless God that my parents did well!

People say, "Well, they just *inherited* money." So what? Bless God for that! I wish I had inherited some money! Y'all act like that doesn't count because they got their money from their parents.

I think it's interesting how people interpret things when they don't understand the way God sees them. If you are successful because you put your hand to the plough, if you believe God and He's increased you, then it is what it is. I am under no obligation to take care of you unless you are in my household!

Now, if I *want* to be a blessing and I *want* to plant seed and give alms in my own personal life, then that's up to me. I direct it as I'm led by the Spirit of God to do so. But to place a demand on someone else is outside of the covenant. This stuff is the Word of God. This is not my opinion!

The owner of the fig tree said, "Cut it down if it doesn't produce." Some people will live off of you for as long as you'll let 'em! Some people have got to get cut off.

"Well, can I *really* do that?" Yes! Yes, you can!

Some people's relationship with you is just because you helped them. They're not trying to help you; you are a supply to *them*. Now, if God told you to do it, that's one thing; but if God didn't say to do it, that's something else!

Are you starting to see a theme developing? God expects production. He expects you to do something, expects you to produce something. He expects you to move. Proverbs has much to say about it. I'll give you a few scriptures and see how you handle it!

PROVERBS 21:25
The desire of the slothful killeth him; for his hands refuse to labour.

Have you ever heard the phrase "champagne tastes and beer pockets"?

Some people talk about all the things they want from God, all the things they're gonna have one day, all the things they're going to do if they hit the lottery. None of them have a plan on how they're going to *make* a million, but they all know what they're going to do if they *get* one! And the truth is that you're not going to get one if you don't have a plan.

When I was a little kid, my friends and I played a game called "That's My Car." We'd stand on the street corner, and when a really nice car would go riding by, the first one who saw it would say, "That's my car!" Then we'd just continue to upscale each other until whoever saw the nicest car won.

That works when you're two years old! That works when you're ten years old!

You can't be 55 and pointing at fancy cars like "That's my car!" That doesn't work.

Everybody wants to go to heaven and nobody wants to die. Everybody wants their champagne tastes; they want to have great things; they want to do wonderful things; they talk about all these grandiose plans, and they're delusions of grandeur.

If you're not willing to get down and do the work, it's not going to happen!

It's so important for us to understand that while God gives you the talent, He expects you to do something with it, not for you to sit back and say, "Well, God, if I'm supposed to be a great leader then increase me as a leader!" No, get yourself some books and learn leadership;

learn how to develop yourself; get out there and do the work; get a job; function and do the things that are necessary to increase who you are so that you can become what God has called you to be.

He expects you to do something with what He gave you! Stop praying and just asking God, "Will you make me a great leader?" No, He already gave you what He's going to give you! It is now your job to go do business with it. It is your job to go function with it. It is your job to increase the very thing on you with your effort! Quit being lazy.

PROVERBS 26:13–16
The slothful man saith, There is a lion in the way; a lion is in the streets. As the door turneth upon his hinges, so doth the slothful upon his bed. The slothful hideth his hand in his bosom; it grieveth him to bring it again to his mouth. The sluggard is wiser in his own conceit than seven men that can render a reason.

A lazy person always has an excuse. They are very quick to give you a reason. If they spent half the time they invest into telling you *why* they're not doing something on *actually doing* what they're supposed to do, they wouldn't be sitting there looking like a sourpuss!

They've got all the answers; that's why they can justify being lazy.

I have a saying about lazy people that I got from my mom: "You couldn't even give them a job in a pie factory eating pies!" Because they're too lazy to even eat the pie!

That's *lazy*. I love me some pie, I have never had a pie that I wasn't gonna eat!

PROVERBS 12:24
The hand of the diligent shall bear rule: but the slothful shall be under tribute.

So many people are like, "I'm tired of working for the man!"

What you're tired of is being a slave, but you don't want to work hard and be a leader.

"I'm tired of working in this type of job. I'm tired of doing this type of stuff!"

Then work hard and become a leader.

"I hate my job! I feel like I'm a slave!"

Work hard and be a leader! When you're lazy, you're going to be a slave, and then you'll be mad that you can't control your own destiny. You'll be mad that you can't decide where you want to go, mad that you can't follow God the way you would like to follow Him.

When you're lazy, you'll always be running around talking about how "If I had it, boy, I would do big things for God!" No, you don't have it because you don't have it.

He said if you want it, if you don't want to be a slave, then work hard and become a leader—or be lazy and be a slave to everything all your life.

PROVERBS 20:4
The sluggard will not plow by reason of the cold; therefore shall he beg in harvest, and have nothing.

You will pay for what you don't do. You might not pay for it immediately, but eventually, you will pay for what you will not handle in its right season. If you want to be successful, you will have to learn that some battles have to be fought now so that you can enjoy their fruits later.

Some people—every time they get a nickel, they spend a nickel. They have nothing stored up for the right season. You know how some of you act when you get your tax return! Never mind paying the bills you owe. You get that tax money and you're like, "Ohhhh, man! I'mma make it *rain* up in this store!" And then two months later, you're submitting a benevolence application because you need the church to pay one of your bills.

It's crazy to think you're going to have a harvest when you need it, when you were too lazy to do what you should have done in the time when you should have done it! And now that there's no harvest, you wanna get up and plough. No, listen, you missed it! The time to plant was in the time to plant so that you would have a harvest *in the time of harvest*. This requires forethought, it requires planning, it requires you to get out in front of this thing!

So many people want to talk about partying and doing the things that they want to do and spending money, but they don't want to work and save up money so that they can enjoy it later. I'm being very honest with you. I do not want to be 70 or 80 years old, wishing I shoulda-coulda-woulda with a life full of regret. When I get to that point in life, I want to decide what I want to do and when I want to do it! If I want to go preach somewhere across the world, then I'll go do that! If God sends me to do it, I'll just go! But if I don't have the Word of God on the matter, if He hasn't said either way, then I want to choose whatever *I* want and not be hamstrung to the place where I wish I had done things earlier in my life and had handled things better.

Not only are lazy people too lazy to do the work, but they're also too lazy even to discern which season they're in. They can't even discern when it's time to work.

When you're 20, you've got all kinds of energy. As you get older, the spirit is renewed day by day, but the body is perishing. If you're reading this and you happen to be in your twenties, when you get to be 40, *things change.*

There was a time when I could eat a whole pizza, drink a whole 2-liter bottle of Pepsi, go to bed, and wake up in the morning and feel just fine! Nowadays, if I eat pizza too close to going to bed, it's a *rough night*! Things change. And you don't want to have to be busting your knuckles at 50, trying to do what a 20-year-old should be doing!

This is why you've got to understand timing and the season you're in. You've got to understand what you're supposed to be doing. You can't be dishonorable and think God's okay with that. You can't dishonor His stuff because you're being lazy.

You can't be like, "Oh, I'm believing God for a new this-or-that, I'm believing God for a job," when you wouldn't eat a pie when it's handed to you. Or when you've mishandled jobs that you've had in the past, where you just wouldn't show up, you treated them with disrespect, and now you want someone to give you a job?

Now you're calling me, "Hey, Pastor, do you know anybody who's hiring?" Yeah, but not for you! Because anybody I call might hire you just because I sent you! Then when you mess up, as I already know you will because you're lazy, it makes me look bad. Now my recommendations and my word aren't trustworthy.

There's an individual who continues to claim to be related to me. They have burned so many different people—I kid you not! People who *know* me, who assume that person is related to me because we have similar names, have extended invitations to them and have gotten burned by them, and they've never said a word to me.

They're thinking, "If they're related, then I don't want to cause strife in the family."

Then when the story comes out (my wife will tell you!), I'm like, "I don't know them!"

They're like, "*Forreal*? He claims to be related!" He's not! And if he is, he's a cousin of a cousin's cousin's nephew two times-removed, never met 'em before, don't know who they are. Don't extend them credit on my behalf, because I don't know them!

God honors what is honorable. There are people whom I could have helped to get a job, but I didn't because they can't even sweep the floor correctly. They can't stick around and help straighten chairs; they're too good for that. They're always trying to find a way to get out of serving.

"I can serve Wednesday, but I can't do this, and I can do this, but I can't do that." And then you want something from me? I'm here all the time! I'll go into the bathrooms and clean them myself if I have to! I'm here to serve. I'm here to do whatever it takes.

Character is everything. And when people give in to laziness, you see it. It's obvious!

"Pastor, come on, help me out." Nope, not today!

Now, when I see that you're on it, you handle things, you're aggressive, you're about it, you are not slothful, you are not a sluggard, you are getting after things, you are producing fruit—I have no problem giving one of my talents to somebody who is producing with their talent!

But if you can't even produce with the talent God gave you, stop looking for anything from anybody else. If you don't regard God, you're just tossing and turning in bed, getting your sleep on! This is the season, this is the time for us to get up and do what we've gotta do. Every one of us has something God has placed inside of us that He desires to use for the kingdom and to make a profit.

Do you know what profit is? It's what's left over when the revenue has exceeded the expenses. Most people don't know what profit really is. They cognitively know, but they really don't *know*—because if you knew what profit was, you would know that you can't live above your means and then call it faith.

"I'm moving by faith." No you're not. You're moving by presumption. You're moving by foolishness. You are unwilling to do what it takes, yet you still want what God has promised.

God promised it to you when you were not lazy. He promised it to you when you put your hand to the plough. He promised it to you when you would do the things He asked you to do in the way He asked you to do them, the way that's in His heart and in His mind.

So you sit around thinking that it's not going to be required of you like it's required of everyone else, which makes you smarter than seven wise counselors, because you know better! You have wise counsel, but you know better than what the wise counsel is telling you!

"What Pastor said can't be true! There's got to be another way!"

You're wiser than seven counselors. I'm reading it straight out of the Bible.

I'm amazed at how many people are so dishonorable toward the things of God. It just blows my mind. I would never think to send a message or to call our church on Sunday morning and say, "I'm not going to be there." I would never think to not show up when I'm supposed to be there.

Can you imagine sitting in church, wondering, "Where's Pastor?" The praise and worship team is singing … and singing … and singing … and singing …. That's actually happened before! Not on my watch, but that's happened before, when we had a guest minister!

He hasn't been back since. You won't leave *my* people sitting there and just say, "Oops!"

I have never done that. I'm where I'm supposed to be. Why?

Because I'm faithful!

When you begin to count things as faithful—that's why I drive the kind of car that I drive. I don't owe anybody a thing, and I don't feel guilty about driving it.

If I see you walking, I might pick you up—or I might not!

Okay, I'm being facetious to a degree. Obviously if you needed a ride, I would give you one. But what I'm trying to help you understand is that so many people think that it's okay to be lazy, and they justify the laziness by the way that they think. They think I owe them something because they refuse to do what I'm willing to do. If you want to be successful, there is a formula to it, and it includes hard work. Wealth is accumulated little by little.

I read a book about the Vanderbilts, one of the United State's wealthiest families since the 1800s even to this day! They're still some of the wealthiest people in the world. When they made investments, all they wanted to make was three percent. They were suspicious of anything more than that! Anything less than that wasn't worth their time.

Multilevel marketing has messed people up, because it's sold a dream that isn't real. Now, if you want to *start* a multilevel marketing company that actually *does* multilevel marketing, I'm in! But if you want me to go around and tell everybody how this swimming cream makes you skinny? I ain't skinny! Stop telling me what your product does when you look a mess.

"Oh, this'll make you skinny!" You're wider than the whole outside! Hold on, dude! You get skinny first!

What you're doing is racing after a dream that you're not really willing to go after yourself. They've sold you on the idea that you're going to get rich quick, but there's only one formula to getting rich— it's called hard work. Somebody did it! Even if you inherited millions of dollars, I guarantee you that your grand-daddy worked hard, and he went against what the world was doing! When the world was resting and sleeping, he was up!

That's why I like getting up at 4 a.m. Nothing's happening at 4 a.m., nobody's bothering you at 4 a.m. (except for a couple of people, but for the most part nobody's up at 4 a.m.) It's my time, I watch the sunrise, think about things, get some work done, while everybody else is sleeping. You want to tell me I haven't *earned* what I have?

Now, if you want to get up, and you want to do what I do, then that's fine! I've had people work with me who were half my age and can't stay with me.

"Pastor, I'm tired." I know! Me too, but bills come around with amazing regularity!

Laziness is never going to lead to success, and the Bible is so clear about it. It's clear about the effort we're supposed to put forth, clear about what God expects.

Ladies, why some of you would want to date a guy who doesn't have a job, I have no idea. They sit at home playing video games all day. I have no idea why you would do that. It is the furthest thing from my mind! When I was single—before I ever really started serving God and all the things I began to know about God concerning my life— when I was a young man, a lot of young men would see a scantily-clad girl, and they would go, "Wow, that's sexy!"

And I would go, "That's not sexy to me."

It never was. I'm being honest with you! Scantily-clad was not the thing that got my goat.

When I saw a woman in a business suit, and she was stepping out of a Mercedes?

I said, "Now *that's* sexy! Being broke is childish and I am quite grown!"

Just because she can wear a bikini does not mean that she knows how to make the money to buy that bikini! So I never understood how a woman could be with a guy who doesn't have a job and doesn't want to work. Now, if there's something physically wrong with him, that's a whole different ballgame. But an able-bodied person? If you don't work, you don't eat.

You are responsible to take care of your family. You can't live in somebody's house and not contribute or tell somebody how they're supposed to do something in the house that you don't pay anything in!

"I don't like the way that you control the TV." I *bought* the TV!

"Well, I have rights, too!" Yes, you have a right to get up and get out! Go get your own job and your own TV in your own house, and then you can watch whatever you want to watch!

It's like these kids nowadays—they're entitled!

"Well, I live in this house, too!" No, you suck up air conditioning in this house. You take up space in this house. You don't *live* in this house until you *pay* for this house. Up until then, you are freeloading!

"I can't believe she took my phone!" You ain't got no phone! Did you buy it? Are you paying for it? No? Then it's not yours! And as long as I'm paying for it, I'll take it from you as I will! I believe in the Golden Rule: He who has the gold makes the rules!

God doesn't like idleness. God expects us to produce, He expects us to be about His business. To just idly sit by and wait? Nothing comes to a sleeper but a dream. If you work and you have no vision for what you're doing, that's a nightmare, and if you dream with no work, you're just daydreaming.

You have to do what it takes to have what God wants you to have. If you expect it to fall out of the sky, think again! If it did fall out of the sky, how do you know it won't hit you in the head? If God drops a

Mercedes out of the sky, you'd better run! Or else you won't be around to drive it!

God expects us to prosper. So don't be lazy—don't be idle.